In true form, this book is littered with magn
like running back to your work and comple
your company's story, if not your own. You will come away from reading
this wanting to connect the head with the heart, and with the certainty
that storytelling is the key to bridging the two. It's a compelling and easy
read with powerful case stories, and a swag of footnotes that will give you
a chuckle along the way.

— **Jenelle McMaster, Managing Partner, Oceania Markets, EY**

There's a lot of gold in this book. *Magnetic Stories* reads like a compelling
story of its own, with clear explanations, relevant examples and practical
outtakes peppered throughout that take you on your own journey to
becoming a better storyteller.

— **Tim Duggan, Author of** *Cult Status: How to build a business*
people adore **& Co-Founder Junkee Media**

A brand, personal or company, really needs to have human connection.
There is no better way for us to connect than through the power of inspiring
and emotive storytelling. Whether communicating your company strategy,
vision, values or just relationship building, an authentic story will resonate
better, be remembered and re-told. *Magnetic Stories* is packed with great
examples of 'case stories' and will give any reader the confidence on how
to create and tell your messages through storytelling.

— **Michael Ebeid, former CEO, SBS, and Group Executive, Telstra**

Thank goodness Gabrielle Dolan doesn't ever run out of things to say,
because every time she writes another book and tells us more stories, her
expertise teaches us further how we can use the power of storytelling for
greater connection and engagement in business.

Written in four parts, sharing the five types of stories businesses need, and
using real life examples from companies around the world, this excellent
'brand storytelling bible' is a magnetic source of inspiration for those who
want to attract commercial success. And check out page 81 if you want to
know where she gets her rockstar shoes from!

— **Jac Phillips, Senior Director and Head of Marketing, Visa**

As 2020 has so acutely demonstrated, we live in an unpredictable and demanding world, where an organisation's brand and their leadership must connect and build trust in a real and meaningful way with their customers and employees. *Magnetic Stories* provides an easily digestible and relevant way to do exactly this across any sized organisation through the use of storytelling.

— **Carrie Hurihanganui, Chief Operating Officer, Air New Zealand**

Gabrielle captivates readers with her use of stories to demonstrate their power. She shows how stories create an emotional connection that helps us remember them and influences decisions. For those who may not yet be convinced of the power of storytelling in building a culture and brand, Gabrielle brings these realities into focus and shares practical tips for implementing storytelling in your organisation.

— **Heather Brilliant, President and Chief Executive Officer, Diamond Hill Capital Management**

The importance of storytelling and being able to paint a memorable and visual mental picture is so important for leaders to connect staff emotionally to the what and the why. *Magnetic Stories* is a useful reminder not to fall into the trap of 'don't let the audience get in the way of my message'. The story should have relevance and meaning. The case studies, examples and questions make for a practical book to use rather than gather dust.

— **Gavin Slater, Managing Director and Chief Executive Officer, Nimble**

Every time I read Gabrielle's wisdom, I am reminded of the need to be more thoughtful in the stories I tell. *Magnetic Stories* reinforces the emotional power of storytelling. It reminds us that stories build deep connections with our stakeholders for the betterment of ourselves as individuals, of teams and of organisations. Gabrielle has hit yet another home run!

— **Gretchen Gagel, Managing Director, Asia Pacific, Conversant**

In my thirty years in business, I have seen many companies struggle with authentically communicating their brand story ... who they are and why we should choose them. Worse still, storytelling is often treated with some suspicion, that somehow being good at storytelling suggests a lack of substance.

And yet the most compelling leaders (and businesses) are those who can really connect with people, inspire them and enrol them in their mission.

In her new book, *Magnetic Stories*, Gabrielle Dolan presents the case for storytelling as an essential skill for connecting with customers and employees, to bring your brand to life. The book is a no-nonsense, accessible 'how-to' guide that uses well-researched case studies to show how successful businesses have built their brand and reputation through stories and actions.

I have seen Gabrielle in action, inspiring and teaching people about the power of storytelling, and she brings that skill and passion to life in this book with an effortless style that is easy to relate to.

Great stories, simple rules and powerful insights – this book is an essential guide for anyone who wants to have a positive impact on their employees and customers and for any business looking to more effectively build their brand through storytelling.

— **Anthony Healy, CEO and Managing Director,**
Australian Business Growth Fund

In *Magnetic Stories* Gabrielle delivers again. Who would have thought that a story about a goldfish could deliver a powerful message about what ownership means or that the story about the creation of a toilet paper manufacturer could be so inspiring (and funny). *Magnetic Stories* is engaging, thought-provoking, easy to digest, littered with humorous asides and, most importantly, practical.

— **Stephen Purcell, Non-executive Chairman, Nexia Australia**

Love this book! Brand storytelling from the inside out is one of the hallmarks of a strong brand. Arm your people with information and inspire them to pass it on.

— **Adam Ferrier, Author of *Stop Listening to the Customer* &**
Founder of Thinkerbell

An enthralling and informative read from cover to cover. The inclusion of so many different company's and people's stories really cemented my understanding of the power of storytelling and how to build a bank of brand stories in my teams.

— **Anne Bennett, Senior Executive**

As someone who has responsibility for nurturing culture within an organisation, Gabrielle's book – *Magnetic Stories* – gave me an inspiring platform from which to creatively engage my staff and ensure a long-lasting culture of storytelling about performance, resilience, and leading by example was left within our firm. Highly recommended for anyone trying to engage their employees on a deeper level.

— **James Bell, Managing Director, Australia and New Zealand, Bloomberg**

In *Magnetic Stories* Gabrielle Dolan again showcases the power of storytelling, especially for 'about us' brand purposes.

This book had me reflecting on how working from home during COVID has provided a window into 'about me' conversations with so many of our team. Their magnetic personal stories have revealed more about our culture and why they want to work for us than any recruitment materials ever could.

Magnetic Stories is a timely reminder of the power of brand stories and a practical guide in how to implement brand storytelling.

— **Lee Scales, Chief Customer Officer, UniSuper Management**

Gabrielle has developed proven and thoughtful communication methodologies that are designed to help leaders succeed in an increasingly cluttered world of long worded mission statements and elaborate values descriptions. Gabrielle convinces the reader that the practice of good storytelling engages us emotionally, connecting the organisation to our personal values.

In *Magnetic Stories*, Gabrielle demystifies the art of storytelling. As a primer on the art of storytelling, chapters are well organised with useful check and reflect prompts, and self-assessment questions. In a world of virtual meetings in the place of face-to-face conversations, Gabrielle's latest book is a fantastic resource in the quest to connect with others in a tangible way.

— **Sarah Williamson, Chief Executive, Antarctica New Zealand**

At a time when connection has never been so important, Gabrielle gives us the gift of sharing and showing us how to craft magnetic stories – ones that stick for our customers and our people. A must-read for all those who want to connect at the heart, not just through facts and logic. Can't wait to take out my highlighter and dog-ear some pages (book sacrilege I know!) and the check and reflect points are a master stroke.

— **Christine Corbett, Chief Customer Officer, AGL**

In *Magnetic Stories*, Gabrielle provides a full picture of how an organisation can not only communicate its brand, but also connect deeply with all kinds of stakeholders through the power of storytelling. Rather than theoretical, Gabrielle uses lots of real stories to demonstrate what it looks like when organisations are doing this. Spanning origin stories, core values stories, customer experience stories, employees' personal breakthrough stories, and stories for the broader community, Gabrielle invites the reader to see the critical role of storytelling in connecting to each of those groups in an engaging, authentic, emotional and relatable way. I especially appreciate her focus on people's personal stories, and how those connect them to an organisation's vision and purpose.

Although my organisation already has a comprehensive story writing program in place, I got a lot of new actionable insights from Gabrielle's book. I saw lots of areas where storytelling was possible, but I hadn't seen it before.

— **Chris Freund, Founder and Partner, Mekong Capital**

magnetic STORIES

magnetic STORIES

CONNECT WITH CUSTOMERS AND ENGAGE EMPLOYEES WITH BRAND STORYTELLING

GABRIELLE DOLAN

WILEY

First published in 2021 by John Wiley & Sons Australia, Ltd
42 McDougall St, Milton Qld 4064
Office also in Melbourne

Typeset in ITC Berkeley Oldstyle Std 11/14

ISBN: 978-0-730-38851-7

A catalogue record for this
book is available from the
National Library of Australia

Cover design by Wiley

Author photo by Oli Sansom

Printed in Singapore by Markono Print Media Pte Ltd

10 9 8 7 6 5 4 3 2 1

Disclaimer
The material in this publication is of the nature of general comment only, and does not represent professional advice. It is not intended to provide specific guidance for particular circumstances and it should not be relied on as the basis for any decision to take action or not take action on any matter which it covers. Readers should obtain professional advice where appropriate, before making any such decision. To the maximum extent permitted by law, the author and publisher disclaim all responsibility and liability to any person, arising directly or indirectly from any person taking or not taking action based on the information in this publication.

For Dad, whose actions created magnetic stories that will be shared for generations to come.

Contents

About the author

Gabrielle can tell you a story or two. In fact, it was while working in a senior leadership role at National Australia Bank that she realised the power of storytelling in effective business communication. Since that epiphany, Gabrielle has found her calling as a global thought leader on real communication and business storytelling.

A highly sought-after international keynote speaker, educator and author, she has worked with thousands of leaders from around the world. Her clients include EY, Accenture, Visa, Amazon, Australia Post, National Australia Bank, Vodafone, Telstra, BlueScope Steel and the Obama Foundation, to name drop a few.

She holds a master's degree in Management and Leadership from Swinburne University, and an associate diploma in Education and Training from the University of Melbourne. She is a graduate of the Harvard Kennedy School of Executive Education in both the Art and Practice of Adaptive Leadership and Women and Power: Leadership in a New World.

Gabrielle is also the best-selling author of *Real Communication: How To Be You and Lead True*, a finalist in the Australian Business Leadership Book Awards for 2019. Her other published books include the chart-topping *Stories for Work: The Essential Guide to Business Storytelling* (2017), which reached number one in Australia's best-selling business books, *Storytelling for Job Interviews: How to Use Stories, Nail an Interview and Land Your*

Dream Job (2016), *Ignite: Real Leadership, Real Talk, Real Results* (2015), which reached the top five on Australia's best-selling business books, and *Hooked: How Leaders Connect, Engage and Inspire with Storytelling* (2013).

Bringing humanity to the way businesspeople communicate isn't just a career, it's a calling. The ultimate expression of her passion for the cause is her Jargon Free Fridays movement that she founded in 2016 as a fun way to raise awareness of the business world's addiction to jargon and acronyms. (Don't ever say the word 'pivot' to her unless you are talking about netball or basketball.)

In 2020, her dedication to the industry was recognised when Gabrielle was awarded Communicator of the Year by the International Association of Business Communicators Asia Pacific region.

She lives in Melbourne with her husband, Steve, and two daughters, Alex and Jess.

gabrielledolan.com

Acknowledgements

As I sit down to write these acknowledgements, my youngest daughter, Jess, is sitting next to me saying, 'Can you mention me first because I am your favourite?' Now parents are not supposed to have favourites (even though we do but to be fair it changes on a daily, sometimes hourly basis). But in all seriousness, I should thank my family first considering they allow me to write so many stories about them. So, to my two daughters, Alex and Jess, and my husband, Steve, thank you for allowing me to openly share your stories. And for supporting me in everything that I do ... and most importantly of being proud of what I do.

Thanks also to my friend and executive manager, Elise Turner, who basically keeps everything chugging along while I am spending long hours writing with a do not disturb sign up. Thank you for all your support, proactiveness, kindness, reliability, attention to detail and friendship.

Massive thanks to Kelly Irving, my editor, whom I have been working with since my first book. I liken writing a book to running a marathon and when I get to about the 15K mark (15 000 words in) and either hit the wall or start going off course, Kelly is there by my side with words of encouragement to get me back on course. We also have an agreement that what happens in the first draft, stays in the first draft ... no-one will ever know how crap that is.

Writing a book is a massive team effort so thanks to the team at Wiley for again having faith in my ideas. To Allison Hiew for doing another round of edits. Plus Lucy Raymond, Ingrid Bond, Bronwyn Evans and Francesca Tarquinio, it is always a pleasure working with you.

Extreme gratitude and respect to the genius of Oli Sansom who took the photo of me for the back cover. He always manages to bring out the best version of me.

Huge thanks to Scott Eathorn who does all the publicity related to the book. His professionalism, follow through and generosity always make it a pleasure to work with him.

Thank you to the people who agreed to read the book and provide a testimonial. Your reviews meant a lot, especially when I was still in the early stages of hoping the book was good.

This book would be very light if it wasn't for the people who agreed to be interviewed for this book. You gave me your time, insights and, most importantly, your stories. I am so grateful that you allowed me to share them to bring the concepts of this book alive.

Finally, thank you to the reader. If you picked up this book you are no doubt an advocate for the power of storytelling. I trust you will find your own magnetic stories while reading this.

Introduction

In 2019 I published my fifth book, and my mother-in-law, Jan, asked me a good question. She asked in a genuinely caring way, 'Don't you run out of things to write about?' I thought about this and agreed that it would be a long, long time before I even considered another book. Yet here I am again.

Here's why.

When I first started my practice on storytelling back in 2005, no-one was talking about storytelling in business. The common reaction I received back then was often along the lines of 'Oh, all that once-upon-a-time stuff?' It was dismissed as not being relevant or credible, or just too emotional and 'touchy feely'.

Fast forward to today, and I never receive this kind of reaction.

PEOPLE REALISE THE POWER OF SHARING STORIES IN BUSINESS AS A RELEVANT, CREDIBLE AND EFFECTIVE WAY TO CONNECT WITH CUSTOMERS AND ENGAGE EMPLOYEES.

So after 15 years of writing and speaking about this topic, you'd think I'd feel like my mission was accomplished. The use of stories in business has gained credibility and popularity. Great. More and more organisations are implementing storytelling. Great. No need for another book ... right?

Well, if you go to the 'Our Story' page on a vast majority of company websites (maybe even yours), you'll realise that, actually, there is no story there at all. It's usually just a bunch of facts, stats and dates, or it's filled with so much verbiage that does nothing but demonstrate an addiction to corporate jargon. You know, 'We incorporate leading-edge design with best-practice methodology to deliver customer-centric solutions in a sustainable manner.'

And what about your 'brand story'—heard of that one? I have clients asking me to help them create their 'brand story' all the time. Yet I can recall writing an article on this over a decade ago titled 'Yeti and the brand story'. (Spoiler alert: neither exist, no matter how hard you try looking.) There is no ONE story that communicates your brand to ALL of your employees and customers.

What is really happening is that the word 'story' is being hijacked … and it's creating even more confusion for people. I've lost count of the amount of times I have read something or listened to someone referring to something as a story and then found myself mumbling, 'but that is not a story'.

A growing number of businesses are attempting to implement storytelling, but they're not doing it very well and are missing out on valuable opportunities to connect and engage employees and customers. From entrepreneurs to small- and medium-sized businesses, to large multinational organisations, there are so many mistakes and sadly a lot of misguided efforts going on.

On the flip side, I have also heard some fabulous stories that have not been shared—even though they absolutely should have been.

THE ONE GOOD THING TO COME OUT OF THE CURRENT CLIMATE IS THE REALISATION THAT HUMAN CONNECTION IS MORE IMPORTANT THAN EVER BEFORE.

COVID-19, Black Lives Matter and the Australian bushfire crisis are just three examples (from 2020 only!) that show how the world has been challenged and is changing.

Our social media feeds are flooded with tragic news, but also with stories of hope. Stories of individuals trying and making a difference, like UK war veteran Captain Tom Moore who at 99 decided to walk 100 laps of his garden before his 100th birthday to raise money for the UK's National Health Service (NHS). His story created such a connection with people that he went on to become a bit of celebrity, raising over £30 million, and he was knighted by Queen Elizabeth II in July 2020.

Then there are stories of companies who responded to the challenges of the coronavirus in unusual and captivating ways, like gin distilleries such as Four Pillars in Melbourne and Archie Rose in Sydney moving production to make hand sanitiser. When hotels around the world were forced to close, two Marriott Hotels in the French Riviera donated their unused produce and food products to a local children's charity.

These stories have been actively communicated by the companies themselves, and they have created a heady mix of magnetism and attraction. We can't help but be drawn to them. They connect with us. They engage us, like never before.

THIS MAGNETIC ATTRACTION IS THE FOUNDATION OF LONG-TERM BRAND LOYALTY.

As such, there are four trends emerging that you need to be aware of when it comes to brand storytelling.

- **Trend 1**: Customers are increasingly making purchasing decision based on their own values. While this is not new, more socially aware consumers are realising their collective power when it comes to influencing companies to make more ethical choices.

- **Trend 2**: Employees are seeking greater alignment between their own personal values and their employers' values. They are looking to work for companies that have a greater purpose than simply profit.

- **Trend 3**: A super-connected world has resulted in a surge of transparency that people are referring to as 'Glass Box Brands'.

Before social media it was more like a black box ... hard to see into and easy to decorate on the outside. Social media has meant it is very hard to hide an internal culture from the outside world.

- **Trend 4**: The birth of 'cancel culture', where people will use social media to call out any company or celebrity that they believe has done something wrong. They will publicly withdraw support and shame them, encouraging others to do the same.

COMPANIES NEED TO BE AWARE OF THE COMBINED IMPACT THESE FOUR TRENDS HAVE ON THEIR BRAND.

The internal and external brand have become one, and it is more important than ever to take control of your brand and your stories.

Hence, this book shows leaders of businesses, from individual to multinational organisations, how to navigate these trends by generating and sharing magnetic stories that authentically engage employees, connect with customers and create brand loyalty.

Your customers and employees can be your greatest brand ambassadors and supporters ... or detractors.

So you need to understand how to choose and use the right stories, in the right way.

In this book, you'll learn how to:

- connect with your customers in a more authentic way

- increase the engagement of your employees

- make decisions based on your company's values and purpose

- champion your employees and customers as your greatest advocates

- take control of your brand and reputation for greater success

- understand the importance of good storytelling (what it is and what it isn't)

- implement brand storytelling effectively

- have a stronger presence online by sharing great stories.

We will focus on the five types of stories you need in business (regardless of size) to connect and engage people with your brand. We'll do this by looking at a diverse collection of real examples to inspire and guide you throughout that process. I will also share with you my proven method to implement storytelling to connect customers and engage employees with your brand.

So, as it turns out, no, Jan, I haven't run out of things to write about, because if there's one thing I've learned, it's that everyone loves a good story but not everyone knows how to find and tell a good one — a magnetic story.

So here goes ...

How to use this book

I very rarely read a business book from cover to cover. Perhaps this influences my style of writing. While you can read this book cover to cover (and I always feel a little bit chuffed when people tell me they do that), you don't have to.

This book has been written in parts, with subsections rather than chapters, and, while it does follow a logical order, you can dip into any part depending on where your interest lies with storytelling.

Part I is all about explaining what brand is and how storytelling is a critical aspect of that. It delves a little bit into the science behind why stories can be so magnetic. A good story can create this immediate attraction to you and your brand which is really hard to pull away from … just like a magnet. Even if you are fully convinced on the power of storytelling, it may still be worth reading this part as it sets up the book and I uncover some really cool insights about heritage, speaking to James Kerr (who wrote *Legacy: What the All Blacks Can Teach Us about the Business of Life*) and Michael Henderson (who wrote *Above the Line: How to Create a Company Culture that Engages Employees, Delights Customers and Delivers Results*).

Part II explores the five different types of stories that you can share in business to engage employees and connect with customers.

These stories are:

1. Creation

2. Culture

3. Customer

4. Challenge

5. Community.

Many companies only focus on one or two of these types of stories and I hope this part of the book, packed with so many different examples of these stories, inspires you to consider them all.

Part III is for the people that are serious about implementing brand storytelling into their organisation. Regardless of the size of the organisation or the industry, the framework I outline in this part of the book will help you implement storytelling effectively. The key word here being 'effectively'. As I discuss in the introduction, one of the driving forces behind me writing this book was because I saw so many businesses attempting to implement brand storytelling but not doing it very effectively.

Part IV came about while I was speaking to companies from around the globe looking for examples of stories. Some companies were doing such interesting things with storytelling that I felt they deserved a bit more air time in the book. The five businesses I showcase here span five different countries and industries, from a baking franchise in Melbourne, Australia, to a restaurant in Florida, USA, an investment company in Vietnam, a power company in New Zealand and an iconic hotel in Singapore.

Feel free to take in this book any way you choose.

PART I

bring together brand and STORIES

So, what is a story and what is it not? How can telling stories help communicate your brand? What does 'brand storytelling' actually mean, and how will it help you connect and engage your customers and employees?

Storytelling is not some airy-fairy kind of fluff. There is some pretty impressive research conducted by neuroscientists around the critical role that story, emotion and memory play when it comes to our actions and decisions. So we'll look at some of these studies to show us why stories are so sticky and how, when used correctly, they can create the kind of magnetic attraction we are talking about.

Let's dig in so you can understand what to do — and what not to do — when it comes to your brand and stories.

The power of brand storytelling

Growing up, I was what everyone would have called a tomboy. I preferred to be outside playing cricket or football or riding my skateboard and BMX bike. I was not into dolls at all. Needless to say, I never owned a Barbie and, decades later, when Barbie was being shamed as not being a good role model for girls, I happily went along with this. I refused to buy my two daughters a Barbie (and I think might even have told others not to buy them one).[1]

Last year, however, I heard the backstory to Barbie and I realised my assumptions had been all wrong.

Barbie's backstory

Ruth Handler was the wife of Elliot Handler, the co-founder of Mattel. She noticed that when her daughter, Barbara, was playing with her paper dolls that she was actually pretending they were adults. In this play, her two children (Ken was their son — yes, Ken and Barbie were named after their children) would act out future events, rather than the present. She also noticed that while Barbara only had dolls that had her playing the role

---

[1] I took a firm stance against gender stereotyping presents or colours. I can still recall getting chastised by my elderly aunt for dressing Alex when she was a baby in a black hat ... which was technically navy blue and did have a red flower on it.

of caregiver, Ken had dolls that encouraged him to imagine himself as a doctor, firefighter, astronaut and so much more.

There were limitations with the paper dolls, including paper clothing that failed to attach well. So Ruth set to work to produce a three-dimensional plastic doll with an adult body and a wardrobe of fabric clothing.

Her husband and other executives at Mattel did not think it was a good idea at all. They assumed parents would not buy their children a doll with a voluptuous adult figure. Basically, a doll that had breasts.

While holidaying in Europe Ruth saw the German Bild Lilli doll and bought one, as it was similar to what she was thinking. She redesigned the doll, named her Barbie, and convinced her husband and the other executives to produce a prototype.

On 9 March[2] 1959, Barbie debuted at the New York Toy Fair and, as they say in the classics, the rest is history.

When you look at the early years of some of the career Barbies that were created, they were actually very progressive. For example, in 1961 we had the Executive Barbie, 1965 Astronaut Barbie, 1973 Surgeon Barbie, 1985 CEO Barbie, 1989 Pilot Barbie. And way back in 1968 Mattel released Equal Rights Barbie, which was one of the first Black dolls on the market.

Ruth Handler is quoted as saying, 'My whole philosophy of Barbie was that through the doll the little girl could be anything she wanted to be. Barbie always represented the fact that a woman has choices.'

The point of this story? Well, it made me connect to Barbie on a whole different level — what about you?

THAT ONE STORY ACTUALLY CHALLENGED AND CHANGED MY VIEW OF THE BARBIE BRAND. AND IT WILL INFLUENCE MY FUTURE BUYING DECISIONS.

That is what a story can do for your brand.

---

[2] My birthday. Not the 1959 bit — just the 9 March bit.

Tales from Europe

Good stories will attract people to your brand, and to your company. These stories drive people to decide to buy your products, to engage your services, to work for you, to recommend you, to support you, to speak favourably about you, to follow you, to refer you, and to keep coming back to you, time and time again.

Stories are so powerful that they can immediately influence purchasing decisions. Here's another couple of good examples I found while on a family holiday in Europe a few years ago.

Story 1: Botas 66

During a guided food tour in Prague, we learned about Botas 66. We had thought they were just an ordinary shoe company, but we soon discovered that they were an iconic Czech brand that make sneakers. The story goes that under communism, they were the only sneakers allowed to be worn. Imagine that? You only had once choice of sneakers to purchase. Once Czech Republic gained independence (again) in 1989, Botas 66 went out of business as people now had a choice. However, two design students resurrected the sneakers in 2007 as part of a school project. They made the sneakers cool by coming up with contemporary designs and colours that still give a retro nod to their heritage. They now have three stores in Prague and over a hundred designs. The word on the street is that you have instant street cred when you wear Botas 66 sneakers. And seriously, who doesn't want street cred?

So we sought out the store and my husband and I bought a pair each.[3]

Story 2: Currywurst sausages

Currywurst sausages are a famous fast food dish in Germany. The story goes that in 1949, care packages were distributed by British soldiers to the people of Germany. One woman received a care package that contained, amongst other things, curry powder and tomato sauce. Not having seen these ingredients before, she mixed them together and served them with a sausage.

---

[3] Not matching, that would be cringe-worthy.

5

Typically, the dish is made from steamed then fried pork sausage, cut into bite-sized pieces and served with fries, mayonnaise, tomato sauce and sprinkled with curry powder. Upon hearing this story from our Berlin guide, we felt compelled to give them a try. The next day we decided to go to the original store that started selling them in 1960. It actually tasted surprisingly better than it looked, but we would never have bothered even trying the dish if it was not for the story![4]

Story 3: Ampelmann

Ampelmännchen is the name for the human figure depicted in the green and red signals at pedestrian lights in Germany. The East Berlin Ampelmännchen, a male figure with a hat, was first installed in 1969 and after reunification in 1990 they started to gradually get replaced by the generic West German Ampelmännchen. This caused protests, and as a result the East German Ampelmännchen was reintroduced in both East and West German cities. As one of the few features of communist East Germany to have survived the fall of the Iron Curtain, it has now become an iconic symbol that adorns a variety of clothing items and souvenirs under the brand Ampelmann.

We were so fascinated by this story and brand that we bought up big in one of their many stores: baseball cap, beanie, t-shirts, socks, lollies, coffee mug, laptop bag, shot glasses, wine glasses and even doormats. Granted, I may have slightly gone overboard — but I did stop short of buying an actual traffic light. (Only because it would have been a bit more difficult to get back home.)

THIS IS THE POWER OF STORIES WITH A MAGNETIC ATTRACTION.

These stories I share over and over, all the time. I don't talk about the facts, or the product benefits, not even the quality of the product.[5]

---

[4] We even arrived 30 minutes before it opened yet still waited.

[5] Although the quality on all was outstanding and the Ampelmann wine glasses were the best I have ever had ... I wish I'd bought more.

Your stories, your brand

If you search the definition of 'brand', you will find an enormous range of terms and phrases that vary greatly. You will also find many articles on how hard it is to define 'brand'.

Marty Neumeier, who is a leading expert on brands and author of such books as *The Brand Gap* and *The Brand Flip*, defines brand by stating what a brand *isn't*: 'A brand is not a logo. A brand is not an identity. A brand is not a product.' Neumeier then adds that 'a brand is a person's gut feeling about a product, service, or organisation'. I like this definition as it implies that brand perception is an emotional gut feeling.

My favourite definition of brand, however, comes from Amazon CEO Jeff Bezos, who is widely quoted as saying, 'Your brand is what other people say about you when you're not in the room.'

My variation of that is:

YOUR BRAND IS THE STORIES PEOPLE SHARE ABOUT YOU WHEN YOU ARE NOT IN THE ROOM.

Brand is the cumulative result of a company's actions. Just like an individual, your brand will be affected negatively or positively by what you do and what you say … not by your intentions, but by your behaviour. (I would love to take credit for that insight, but it was the great Dr Stephen Covey who said, 'We judge ourselves by our intentions and others by their behaviour.')

A company's actions are determined by a combination of the company's culture, values, desired behaviours, purpose, vision, mission and strategy. Every organisation will have different names for all of these, but collectively they are their brand because they influence how people behave.

Throughout this book, when I refer to 'brand' I am using this as an overarching word for culture, values, behaviours, strategy, purpose, mission and vision.

If a company values 'win at all costs' over 'fairness and doing the right thing', that will influence employee behaviour and therefore the company brand.

If a company has a vision statement to be the 'most profitable in the industry' as opposed to the 'most respected in the industry', that will influence their behaviour and therefore their brand.

This might be the behaviour of the CEO in a press conference, or the call centre person answering enquiries.

EVERY SINGLE EMPLOYEE IN EVERY ORGANISATION CAN AFFECT THE BRAND POSITIVELY OR NEGATIVELY, EVERY SINGLE DAY.

When you think about how you feel about a particular company and the stories you share about it, they are normally based on a positive or negative interaction you have personally had or a positive or negative story you have heard.

The reality is people are already sharing stories about you, whether you know it or not ... and regardless of whether you like those stories or not!

This applies to individuals as well as any business ... whether you are a small, one- or two-person company or a large multinational; a not-for-profit or a government organisation; a start-up or a corporate institution; a school or a sporting team; a religious institution or a political party; a local café or a global franchise ...

Your employees share stories about you. So do your past employees, your potential employees, your customers, your potential customers, your competitors, your suppliers, your partners, your stakeholders ... and so on.

IT IS NEVER TOO EARLY OR TOO LATE TO START TAKING CONTROL OF YOUR BRAND ... ALTHOUGH I AM A STRONG BELIEVER THAT THE EARLIER YOU DO IT THE BETTER.

I mean, if the stories people share about you define your brand, then wouldn't you want to have some influence over those stories?

What is brand storytelling?

Using stories to communicate your brand is often referred to as 'brand storytelling'. Sometimes it's helpful, when defining what something is, to define what it is not. So, as Marty Neumeier said, it is not about a logo or a product. Brand storytelling is also not a tagline, or a timeline of your company. It's not a slick corporate video or a TV commercial. It's not a brochure or your purpose, vision and values stated on a page. And it is definitely not just one story.

It's a combination of lots of stories.

It's a deliberate approach to find and share stories, both internally with your employees and externally with your customers … and others.

It's about being very clear on what your brand is and using stories to attract people to that brand.

To me, brand storytelling is a deliberate and sustainable approach to authentically communicate your brand, internally and externally, through the stories you share and the stories people share about you based on your actions and behaviours.

It's not an easy process and it's not quick.

BUT DONE RIGHT, DONE AUTHENTICALLY, IT CAN STRENGTHEN YOUR ORGANISATION AND HELP YOU ATTRACT AND RETAIN TALENTED EMPLOYEES AND LOYAL CUSTOMERS.

So, we'll look at the science behind that attraction next.

A magnetic attraction

On the same holiday I mentioned previously, I visited the Stasi Museum in Germany. My husband, Steve (who would happily spend a vast amount of time in museums), and elder daughter, Alex (who is studying International Studies and Politics at university), were thrilled about the trip. On the other hand, our younger daughter, Jess, was coerced into going with the promise of a shoe-shopping expedition afterwards, and I was fine as long as it was a 90-minute visit and not an all-day event.

The Stasi Museum documents the influence of the German Democratic Republic Secret Service from 1950 to 1989. The layout of the museum is typical, with displays, images and text explaining their significance. Along the walls were the timelines of what happened in each year.

Jess and I stayed close to each other in order to make our own early secret escape to the café downstairs. Before our departure, we went into every room reading the information: mostly dry facts with an unbelievable number of acronyms. After a while Jess said to me, 'I am reading everything, but nothing is entering my brain.' Can you relate to this? I certainly could!

However, then we came to one room that had stories of individuals who were personally affected by the Stasi. For example, one woman recounted how she was targeted with personalised psychological attacks. This included entering her house and moving things around when she wasn't there, or letting her bike tyres down while she was doing her grocery shopping. She said the incidents were bizarre things that 'no-one would believe'. Consequently, if you mentioned it to anyone, they would think you were either paranoid or mad.

Another man shared a story about receiving continuous anonymous letters about his wife having an affair. He knew it was the Stasi's attempt to destroy his family by eroding trust in their personal relationships.

Jess and I stayed in this room and read every single story. We stayed in that particular room longer than any of the other rooms.

SUFFICE TO SAY, THE STORIES NOT ONLY ATTRACTED US, BUT ALSO MAINTAINED OUR ATTENTION.

And here is why that happened.

Made for memory

Neuroscientist Carmen Simon is the author of *Impossible to Ignore: Creating Memorable Content to Influence Decisions*. Her research shows that the whole purpose of the brain is to make decisions. Do we stay or go? Do we go this way or that way? Reading this very sentence, you are subconsciously deciding whether to keep reading the next sentence or to put the whole book down.

Simon's research shows that every decision is based on memory. We don't touch a flame because we know from memory that it can burn. We don't eat chilli because we know from memory that it doesn't agree with us. We don't drink too much alcohol because we know the next day we will get a hangover.[1]

The research also showed that 'people act on what they remember, not on what they forget'. And that for us to remember anything it first needs to grab our brain's attention. Consequently, the main reason we don't remember stuff is because it didn't grab our attention in the first place!

---

[1] Okay, often we forget that bit or are prepared to suffer the consequences.

For example, when I was 17, my brother-in-law drove me to work every day for two months. Then I got my licence and drove myself for the first time ... and got hopelessly lost. Why? Because all the trips beforehand I was not paying attention. Has this ever happened to you?

'Death by PowerPoint' is another example of this. When we sit in presentations full of bullet points after bullet points, we are bored because nothing grabs our attention.

It's often only when someone shares a story (a real, relevant story) that it gets our attention and we remember it. Most of the time, the story is potentially the only thing we remember.

CAN YOU RECALL A GREAT SPEAKER YOU SAW YEARS AGO? WHAT DO YOU REMEMBER FROM THEIR PRESENTATION? CHANCES ARE IT'S THEIR STORY, OR A STORY THEY SHARED.

As Simon's research proves, we need to engage the brain first, to get its attention, which then leads to memory, which then leads to a decision.

As Simon says,[2] 'Your buyer's decision to purchase will happen in the future, but you can influence those decisions in your favor now.'

When we talk about buyers, we mean more than in the literal sense of buying a product or service. Yes, that is important, but it also refers to people deciding to work for you, recommend you, invest in you, follow you or defend you.

Draw on emotions, not logic

If you've read any of my previous books then you likely will have heard about some crucial research by neuroscientist Antonio Damasio, showing how emotion plays a significant role in our ability to make decisions. (But just in case you haven't I'm going to tell you about it again here.)

---

[2] See what I did there?

While many of us believe logic drives our choices, the reality is that we have already made an emotional decision and we then use logic to justify the choice — to ourselves and to others.

Damasio's research involved examining people with damage to their frontal lobe, which is the area of the brain that generates emotions and helps to regulate personality. Except for their inability to feel or express emotions, the participants had normal intellectual capacity in terms of working memory, attention, language comprehension and expression. However, they were unable to make decisions.

The vast majority of participants could describe in logical terms what choice they thought they should make, but they found it difficult to actually make a decision, including simple ones like deciding what to eat. This indecision came from them going over the pros and cons for each option again and again. Presented with a choice, we struggle to make a decision without some form of emotion influencing it.

This is the reason why stories have such a magnetic ability — an ability to stick in our memory and then sway our decisions. They draw on our emotion, not just on logic, data and bullet points.

Daniel Goleman, author of the best-selling book *Emotional Intelligence*, explains that our brain's neocortex is the reason our emotions are so powerful. The emotional centre of the brain can actually 'influence the functioning of the rest of the brain'.

Good stories make us feel something as we listen to them, whether that's excitement, fear, anger or enthusiasm. Consequently, we feel something towards the person telling the story, which helps create connection.

THE SAME EFFECT CAN HAPPEN WHEN COMPANIES SHARE STORIES. IT CAN HELP CREATE AN EMOTIONAL CONNECTION, AN ATTRACTION TO YOUR BRAND.

In Tim Duggan's 2020 book *Cult Status: How to Build a Business People Adore* he stated,

> *If you're not controlling the message and telling your story, your intended audience can't create an emotional connection with you that builds trust and empathy and creates the potential for a cult brand.*

Pulling power

The research in this chapter proves that tapping into emotion not only aids our understanding of a logical message, but also helps us retain that information. We are more likely to remember a good story as opposed to a bunch of facts, because a story makes us feel something.

As American poet Maya Angelou famously said, 'People will forget what you said. People will forget what you did. But people will never forget how you made them feel.'

AND THAT FEELING CAN BE LONG LASTING. LIKE A MAGNET, ONCE THERE IS A CONNECTION, IT CAN BE VERY HARD TO PULL AWAY FROM IT.

'Just give me the story!'

'Tell me the facts and I'll learn. Tell me the truth and I'll believe. But tell me a story and it will live in my heart forever.'

If this Native American proverb is true, then why in business do we have such a bias towards facts? Why do we communicate and influence with data points, graphs, bullet points and all the boring stuff, and largely ignore stories?

Why is it that we've heard 'Just give me the facts' many times in our career and have probably never heard 'Just give me the story'?

Don't get me wrong: data is important in business, and logic and facts are critical for credibility and judgement, but, as the previous chapter demonstrates, they don't inspire or influence in the same way stories do.

The reality is we need both. Yet we have a misguided bias towards facts. An example of this is if you look at the 'About Us' section on a company's website, annual report or sometimes even in the foyer of their head office. It's usually a list of dates and significant events about how and when the company was formed.[1] But these efforts in documenting and communicating this history are often misguided. While this history could be interesting to some, it rarely helps us connect and engage our employees and customers. Unlike our heritage.

---

[1] By the way, changing the name from 'About Us' to 'Our Story' does not make it a story.

HERITAGE AND HISTORY ARE BOTH IMPORTANT, BUT WHILE HISTORY TENDS TO EDUCATE AND INFORM, HERITAGE HAS THE POWER TO CONNECT AND INFLUENCE.

Heritage over history

To help explain what I mean here, I'd like you to introduce you to my favourite anthropologist of all time. Well, unfortunately, Indiana Jones was not available, so I contacted my favourite *corporate* anthropologist, Michael Henderson.

Michael has over 25 years' experience working with corporates on their culture. He has authored eight books on organisation culture, leadership and performance, including *Get Tribal* and *Above the Line*. He was born in the UK, raised in Africa and educated in New Zealand.

I have had the privilege of seeing Michael present on several occasions and have discussed all things storytelling and culture with him over a few glasses of wine. I spoke to Michael specifically for this book via Zoom on a cold winter's morning.[2]

Michael shared with me that the word 'heritage' comes from the Latin word *hereditatem,* meaning 'to inherit'. This can be in the form of money, land and objects — or it could be in the form of tradition. 'History is all about the facts and heritage is all about the stories,' Michael explained.

Like me, Michael believes that heritage stories are often overlooked in many organisations. To explain why this is something that needs to be rectified, let's look at how heritage works.

Michael shared with me the background of the *Seanchaí* (pronounced shan-a-key), who were traditional Irish storytellers. Through their stories they were the custodians of history for centuries in Ireland. Their role was to be the carriers of folklore, to recite ancient lore and tales of wisdom. Michael describes this as providing a 'profound cultural gift'.

---

[2] I was disappointed he was wearing a beanie as opposed to a fedora like Indy.

You see successful examples of traditional storytellers in other cultures too: the Australian Aboriginal and New Zealand Māori elders, for example. They pass on wisdom to ensure the culture is not lost. These Indigenous peoples, as well as religions around the world, rely on the use of stories to communicate their beliefs and customs. Even the word 'folklore' means the traditional beliefs, customs and stories of a community, passed through the generations by word of mouth.

We often encounter examples of this folklore while travelling. Take Ireland's Blarney Stone, a popular tourist attraction. Apparently kissing the stone endows the kisser with the gift of the gab. No-one really knows if this is true, hence why you will often see it written or told as 'according to legend'. But the story is so powerful it is communicated and passed on regardless.

I'm sure you've been somewhere in the world and thrown a coin into a fountain or rubbed a statue to 'bring you luck'. For example, Abraham Lincoln's nose in Oak Ridge Cemetery; the boot of the John Harvard statue at Harvard University; or even the testicles on the Charging Bull statue just off Wall Street in New York.

Are these stories true? Do they really bring you good luck? Who knows, but it's the story that has a magnetic pull for us. I've been to the John Harvard statue in the grounds of Harvard University. The statue itself is mounted on a big concrete block about 180 centimetres tall, with his boot hanging over the edge. I did not have any evidence at all that rubbing the toe would bring me good luck, yet I rubbed it anyway ... because the story made it real. (I have also been to the Charging Bull in New York but stopped short of rubbing the testicles ... too weird.)

As times goes by, it's the stories that make things real, not the actual event. Michael says that over time, 'Stories move beyond the truth ... beyond the actual facts.'

Stories that stand the test of time

Now, I'm not suggesting you just make stuff up, but as Michael's work shows us, over time the story is what makes it real for a whole new generation. The story is what people connect and engage with. Without the ongoing sharing of the story, the actual event will be lost and forgotten.

For example, have you heard the story of Roger Corbett, the retired CEO of Woolworths, and a shopping trolley? (No, it's not a joke.) Apparently when he was running Woolworths' retail operations in 1998 he came across an empty Woolies trolley and pushed it all the way from Sydney's Circular Quay near the Opera House to the Town Hall supermarket: a 1.5-kilometre trip.

At the time, Corbett was creating a culture of attention to detail and cost reduction. He retired in 2006, yet that story is still shared today; it's formed part of the Woolworths heritage.

The other story I often hear comes from when Apple was developing the very first iPod. Apparently when engineers completed the prototype, they showed it to Steve Jobs for his approval. Jobs was not happy, saying it was too big. The engineers explained that it was simply impossible to make it any smaller. Jobs responded by dropping it in a fish tank and as the air bubbles floated to the top, he said, 'Those are air bubbles so it means there's space in there. Make it smaller.'

I also think Steve Jobs knew a thing or two about the power of stories, considering this quote is attributed to him: 'The most powerful person in the world is the storyteller. The storyteller sets the vision, values and agenda of an entire generation that is to come.'

Generations on, people are still kissing the Blarney Stone in Ireland, and rubbing parts of a statue to bring good luck, and will continue to do so for generations to come. Likewise, the stories of Roger Corbett and Steve Jobs can still influence the vision, values and agenda of an entire generation that is to come.

You can too, if you use the right stories.

The value of heirlooms

Heritage stories can be created from behaviours, such as Corbett returning the trolley and Jobs dropping the iPod in the fish tank, but they can also be associated with heirlooms. Remember the word 'heritage' comes from the word 'inherit': often there is a valuable story behind something that has been passed on in your company.

My father recently passed away and as Mum cleared some of his belongings out, she asked us if we wanted anything. It was amazing that what held no significance to one sibling held enormous significance to another. From card holders he'd had made for him and his friends when they would play cards every Saturday night after church, to a jewellery box he'd made, to his old set of screwdrivers. They have no monetary value, but the story is what gives them value.

THE STORY CONNECTS AND CREATES VALUE FOR THE AUDIENCE.

During lockdown throughout the coronavirus pandemic, there was an increase in social media challenges asking people to post a travel photo a day for 10 days without explanation. Or a music album that meant something to them but again without explanation. I found these infuriating because without the backstory, it doesn't mean anything.

Michael shared with me a time years ago when he worked in a call centre in London for a magazine that sold cars:

> *In the lobby a fake campside fire sat in the middle of the floor, as the first executive team meeting had taken place around a fireplace. The fire symbolised equality for all, as people sitting around a fire can all see each other and hear one another. The story of the fire was referred to in every sales meeting and in all induction programs and award ceremonies in every branch nationwide.*

The fake campfire was a way of keeping the story alive, connecting current employees with the company values demonstrated in a meeting that took place years earlier. So much more powerful than just stating 'we value equality' … the story creates the connection.

Rituals help tell stories

It's not only stories behind heirlooms that can provide connection, it's also stories behind rituals. Take for example the New Zealand All Blacks rugby team and the haka they perform before every game. During the 1980s the All Blacks almost stopped performing the haka because the current players had lost the connection to what it meant. They felt like they were going through the motions.

Michael, who has studied the All Blacks in his work, said:

> Captain Wayne (Buck) Shelford and his Māori colleague Hika Reid said in 1985, 'We either stop doing it or do it properly and understand what it means.' They voted to do it properly, so Buck taught them how. The haka has since become a central and grounding ritual of the team that has the highest winning percentage of any sports team in any sports code across multiple seasons.

In James Kerr's book *Legacy: What the All Blacks Can Teach Us about the Business of Life*, he says, in relation to the haka and rituals, 'Inspiring leaders establish rituals to connect their team to its core narrative, using them to reflect, remind, reinforce and reignite their collective identity.'

I interviewed James about the importance of the stories behind the rituals and he agreed that 'without the story the ritual loses its power'. In fact, in *Legacy* he explores a later time when the All Blacks almost stopped doing the haka again. In 2005, many of the players felt that it had become more about the spectacle and they had lost a personal connection with it. They went through the process of involving all the players to co-create a new haka, with new actions and words. James says that the 'output was a new haka but the outcome was a new connection' and that they had 'revitalised a heritage story'.

James also explains how the most senior players always sweep the sheds after each game. The story goes that after having a few post-game beers the then assistant coach Steve Hansen noticed how untidy the shed was and started to clean it up. The players that were still there started to help him. It got to the point where they would tell the cleaners they would clean up themselves. It's part of their culture of leaving something better than you found it and their value of humility.

Leave a legacy

A ritual does not have to be hundreds of years old to be part of your heritage; there are modern heritage stories. James believes that the role of leaders is to create stories today for tomorrow, as that can leave a legacy.

Very few companies focus on their heritage and share stories that create a connection to an event that has happened in the past (even the recent past) or an heirloom or ritual that has been passed on ... very few.

OUR BIAS TOWARDS FACTS OVER STORIES PREVENTS ORGANISATIONS FROM SUCCESSFULLY COMMUNICATING THINGS THAT MATTER, WHICH CAN CREATE A MAGNETIC ATTRACTION.

This is why when we step into a professional situation — when we walk through those revolving doors, set up a company website, write a quarterly newsletter, design an induction program, create a social media campaign, or place an artefact from the past in the foyer — we need to share the stories, not just the facts.

So, next time someone says to you 'Just give me the facts', respond with, 'Sure — and how about I throw in a magnetic story as well?' You will at least get them intrigued.

That's why in the next part of this book we are going to look at the five types of magnetic stories you should consider finding and sharing to create a magnetic attraction and lasting impact.

PART II

tell
5 types
of brand
STORIES

Brand stories are more than a slick corporate video or a timeline on your website. They are also more than one type of story. They should be many, and they should be varied.

But what, then, are those stories you should be telling your customers and your employees?

In Part II, I'll provide you with examples of five different types of stories you should consider sharing to communicate your brand.

1. **Creation stories** of how and why your organisation started.

2. **Culture stories** of employees living the company values or sharing what those values mean to them.

3. **Customer stories** that showcase your customers to amplify their voice.

4. **Challenge stories** of how the organisation has responded to both internal and external challenges ... big or small.

5. **Community stories** of how the company is fulfilling its corporate responsibility and doing good things to help the community.

Let's take a look.

CREATION STORIES
HOW AND WHY IT ALL STARTED

A couple of years ago, I purchased some swimwear for my husband for his birthday. They were tailor-made out of recycled fishing nets. Since he's a fisherman and someone who hates baggy board shorts, I knew they would be a hit (which they were). I noticed on the company's website there was a tab for 'Our Story', so obviously I clicked through to have a read. Now, as far as 'our stories' go on websites it wasn't bad, but I instinctively thought there would be a more interesting story about why the company started. I mean, it's a pretty unique idea, don't you agree?

I contacted the owner. It turns out that she spent a lot of time at the beach after the birth of her third child. She noticed that women had a large variety of options when it came to swimwear, yet men seemed to have a choice between tight speedos or baggy board shorts ... and not much in between. It was during that time, while taking a break from her other job, that she started designing tailored swimwear for men, and came to the idea of using recycled fishnets through her interest in sustainability and recycling.

This to me was a far more intriguing story than what was on their website.

Most organisations tend to have a pretty interesting story behind why they were created. But in many cases they are reluctant to share it for a variety of reasons.

First, I think a lot of small organisations want to appear bigger than they are; they avoid sharing the founder's story, believing it will make them come across as a small operation.

Second, they don't think it's relevant or that people will be interested in it, which couldn't be further from the truth, as this example shows.

Finally, with so many bad examples of timelines and marketing blurbs called 'Our Story', it's easy to think that this is just what we do!

So it's time to share some good creation stories from real companies so you can get inspired, go away and write your own, too.

Do you give a crap?

This is a toilet-paper manufacturing company originally started by three guys in Melbourne, Australia, which has now spread to the United States. Here is their story on the 'About Us' of their website, which I love.

> Sure, we love puppies and sunny days and walks on the beach, but our real love is toilet paper. Why, you might ask?
>
> First of all, it's funny. Lots of room for toilet jokes, which we love.
>
> But really, we love toilet paper because for us, it's our way of making a difference. We started Who Gives A Crap when we learnt that 2.3 billion people across the world don't have access to a toilet. That's roughly 40% of the global population and means that around 289 000 children under five die every year from diarrhoeal diseases caused by poor water and sanitation. That's almost 800 children per day, or one child every two minutes.
>
> We thought that was pretty crap. So in July 2012, Simon, Jehan and Danny launched Who Gives A Crap with a crowdfunding campaign on IndieGoGo.

Simon sat on a toilet in our draughty warehouse and refused to move until we had raised enough pre-orders to start production. 50 hours and one cold bottom later, we'd raised over $50 000.[1]

We delivered our first product in March 2013 and have been thrilled to keep growing ever since. Not just because our toilet paper is gracing bathrooms across the country but also because we donate 50% of our profits to help build toilets and improve sanitation in the developing world.

Though we're still growing, and now make more than just toilet paper, we always want to stay true to our roots: toilet humor and making the world a better place.

Two girls and a gin still

Kim Seagram is the co-founder and co-owner of Abel Gin, a boutique gin distillery based in Launceston, Tasmania. She was born and raised in Canada but moved when she was 28 after falling in love with a Tasmanian when they met on a ski trip in Canada.

I met Kim through the International Women's Forum that we are both members of. After hearing about her and the gin she produced I checked out their website. I noticed on the website they had 'Our Story', so, unable to help myself, I went in to see if it was actually a story or not ... thankfully it was, and a good one at that! I decided it warranted inclusion in this book. I also thought I'd better purchase some gin ... for research purposes, of course.

Two girls and a still ... Natalie, as we know, is a sparkling wine and distilling guru ... Kim's just a bit of a lush but she comes by it honestly. Her great great grandfather Joseph E Seagram started up Seagram's, once the world's largest producer of alcohol, all from a still at the back of a general store in Canada. Yes, her name is Seagram, and although they don't have a general store, their still is in the back of an old airport shed!

---

[1] You can see the video on YouTube by searching 'Who Gives A Crap toilet paper — First Edition'.

Allow us to reintroduce ourselves

While researching for this book, I was introduced to Anuroop Kumar and Lionell Ball. They shared with me the story of how they started their company, Inflect Digital. It's a story that they share with every client when they meet them for the first time, and include on their proposal:

Allow Us to Reintroduce Ourselves ...

After consulting over $100 million in Facebook ads, Inflect Digital was created when, one afternoon, we were discussing how most agencies were not providing transparency and value for their clients.

Working for Facebook, we had the opportunity to speak with prominent marketing executives, agencies, and entrepreneurs every day. We consulted them on how to optimise their ad campaigns, how to scale their ads, how to retarget customers stuck in their funnel, and how to best allocate their ad budgets. But we also discovered one more thing. ... Most agencies didn't know what they were doing. They implemented techniques they read on a blog somewhere online or heard from someone in a group. There was an incredible 'herding' around ideas and a lack of innovative solutions tailored to client needs.

We figured out that there was this herd mentality because people didn't know what in the world was happening on the backend. That was our cue. We moved forward with Inflect Digital, carrying a vision that we would provide an elite level Facebook ads service to businesses without over-charging them.

Our friends still think we're delusional; but one successful campaign after another — we are determined to continue proving them wrong!

Warmest,

Anuroop & Lionell

When I spoke to Anuroop and Lionell, I asked them if they had company values. Their eyes lit up and responded with an 'absolute yes'. They explained that when they left Facebook to start their own company they were passionate about ensuring the way they ran their business was aligned with their personal values: quality, sincerity, transparency and problem solving.

They talked about being really transparent with their clients. About always coming from a position where they continually develop themselves so they can provide thought leadership, data-driven processes and marketing automation to help their clients solve problems with better efficiency.

Their creation story communicates these values.

A very good reason to drink

A similar type of story comes from Australian company Goodwill Wine, founded by David Laity. The story on their website not only covers why the company was founded but, in the process, shows what they stand for.

> Ten years ago, I lost most of what I owned in the Black Saturday bushfires. I was grateful to be alive and very humbled at how Australians stepped up to help.

> Because of the money you dropped into donation tins around the country, I was able to start again. With a powerful new motivation to drive me on, I made it my mission to 'pay forward' the incredible generosity shown to me.

> I started a business that gave back 50% of everything I earned, and I gave it to the charities my customers cared most about. I loved wine, and I had awesome contacts at some great vineyards who agreed to help.

> And so with the $15 000 given to me by people like you, Goodwill Wine was born.

> Since then, Goodwill Wine has given back $400 000. This money has:

> - Bought fire-fighting equipment, hi-vis wet weather gear and defibrillators for volunteer fire brigades.

> - Provided over 180 000 meals for people living in poverty here in Australia.

- *Funded four International Animal Cruelty Investigations for Animals Australia.*

- *Helped re-home 47 orangutans.*

- *Played a role in introducing a plastic bag ban in Queensland.*

- *De-sexed, vaccinated, microchipped, wormed and re-homed over 100 dogs and 150 cats.*

- *Saved 12 Whales for Sea Shepherd by paying for fuel for their Southern Ocean campaigns.*

We employ disadvantaged Australians. Half of our team come from either long-term unemployment or are living with a disability.

We couldn't have done any of this without you and this is just the start. Our aim is to donate more than one million dollars to charity — by selling quality wine at below cellar-door prices.

Because I'm picky about what wines to sell, I've built a loyal customer base of wine lovers who keep coming back. With each purchase, 50% of the profits goes to charity.

Want your next bottle of wine to help make the world a better place?

Start shopping now! And thanks for reading to the end.

If you ever needed justification to drink some wine, this is it.

I contacted David to ask about the impact the story has had and he informed me that 'it has played a major part of the business and growth of the business'. He also confided that he wanted to stop sharing the story stating that he 'felt a tremendous amount of guilt in surviving the bushfires, when many didn't'. And that guilt was compounded because he has managed to turn a tragedy into a positive.

David realised, however, that his customers really connected to the story, so he said, 'I just chose to embrace it.' But he is aware that what the company is now is 'bigger than his story' and why he started the company. He believes the stories about how they are making an impact are also what customers really connect with, and what his growing number of employees get excited about.

David advised that recently, as the company has expanded with the help of some angel investors, they have been able to do more advertising. As an experiment, they ran an advertisement on Facebook and Instagram with the story they have on their website (as mentioned previously).

David said the results were staggering and it was their most successful advertisement campaign ever. It converted at twice the rate of their second-best conversion ad and drove traffic to the website at a third of the cost of their second-highest-traffic ad.

The company now makes a conscious effort to not lose these stories of the impact they are making to the charities they support. They do this by sharing them in newsletters and blogs.

I was so glad that David decided to embrace his story and keep it as an important part of the company's brand. Many companies feel the need to move beyond the founder's story as they grow. Perhaps the founder thinks similarly to David, in that the company has moved on and is bigger or more than just that one story. And, of course, a company is bigger than one story. A brand is more than one story.

HOW THE COMPANY STARTED AND WHY THE COMPANY STARTED SHOULD ALWAYS FORM PART OF A COMPANY'S BRAND. IT SHOULD NEVER BE FORGOTTEN.

We all started somewhere

Even the biggest companies in the world all started somewhere. Relatively young companies such as Google, Virgin, Facebook, Microsoft, Amazon and Apple all have the founders playing a major role in the brand of the company. Even after Steve Jobs's death he is still a major part of Apple's brand.

There are a lot of institutions in this world that have been around for what feels like forever. I did a search on the oldest companies to see what stories I could dig up and this is what I found.

The Royal Mint was established in 886, so is over a thousand years old. It was started by Alfred the Great when he recaptured London and began issuing silver pennies bearing his portrait.

Then there is Staffelter Hof, a winery and guesthouse in Germany that has been operating for over 1150 years. The land was originally owned by the Carolingian Dynasty from 580 to 876 AD, when they donated the land to the local abbey for them to work and earn income. It stayed in the possession of the abbey for 942 years, until it was purchased by the current family in 1805 and has subsequently passed down seven generations to the current wine maker, Jan Matthias Klein. (Wow!)

I had to search for these stories, but it didn't take me that long. I wish it had been as simple as looking on their website! Unfortunately, I had to find them from different resources. In fact, the 'history' tab on the Staffelter Hof website took me back to the Wikipedia page! Such a missed opportunity, because I found the story really interesting.

SO IF YOU THINK THAT YOUR STORY ISN'T COMPELLING ENOUGH OR THAT YOU DON'T HAVE ONE, THEN THINK AGAIN AND MAYBE TAKE UP THE CHALLENGE TO FIND IT AND SHARE IT.

Check and reflect

- Do you know how and why your company started?

- If not, could you find out?

- If you do know, is that story worth sharing?

- Where could you share the creation story?

- Do all new employees know why the company started?

- If the founder of the company is no longer involved, is it still worth sharing their story?

CULTURE STORIES
OUR VALUES AND BEHAVIOURS ... THE VIBE

You will often hear people describe their workplace as having 'a great culture' or a 'toxic culture' and not really be able to articulate it beyond that ... just that 'you know if it's the right fit for you or not'. Sound familiar?

It reminds me of the words Dennis Denuto shares in the iconic Australian movie *The Castle* when he is trying to sum up his case for the judge: 'It's the constitution. It's Mabo. It's justice. It's law. It's the vibe ... that's it. It's the vibe. I rest my case.'

When we refer to culture, what we are really talking about (aside from the vibe) are the values and behaviours of a group of people. That could be a business, a sporting club or your own family. There is a certain set of values and rules that people in this group are expected to live by.

COMPANY VALUES NEED TO BE COMMUNICATED IN SUCH A WAY THAT PEOPLE UNDERSTAND AND ENGAGE WITH THEM.

The issue is that the standard approach to communicating values seems to be to print them on every available surface, especially coffee mugs and even mouse pads back in the day.

Normally, cultural change programs in larger organisations involve coming up with a new purpose, new values, new behaviours, and 'rolling them out', often changing with the appointment of a new CEO. If you have been in business for a while you have probably gone through your fair share of values 'roll-outs'. You may even have a collection of mouse pads and coffee mugs to prove it.

In smaller companies and start-ups, on the other hand, usually the culture evolves from the initial founder or founders.

I strongly believe that the only way you can communicate values is with stories. Not with coffee mugs, not with mouse pads, not with bullet points listed under each value explaining what it means.

There are two types of stories when it comes to communicating your culture.

1. **Personal connection stories.** These are stories that come from personal experience (not work related) that generally the senior leaders share to communicate what the company's values mean to them personally. It helps them create a personal connection to a company value when they communicate what the values mean to their teams.

2. **Living the values stories.** These are stories that the organisation's leaders share about how they or their employees are living the values, highlighting what they have done that shows what that value looks like in reality.

Let's look at the first one because this is where most companies get implementing storytelling wrong.

Personal connection stories

While researching for this book, I put the call out to a large number of communication specialists around the globe for examples of culture stories. The initial signs were promising. I would be sent links to videos titled 'Our Stories' or something similar.

What I saw in most cases, however, was beautifully shot videos of employees talking about what a particular value meant to them. For example, if the value was 'ownership', they would explain, 'This means to take responsibility for your decisions and actions. It means admitting your mistakes', or perhaps they would say, 'It's about doing what you say you will do.' So while these videos talk about what the value is and means, it's not a story. They were not sharing a personal story to communicate what the company value meant to them, yet they were calling them 'stories'.

To demonstrate what I mean, let's look at someone who does use a story to communicate what 'ownership' means.

Cough the Fish

Emma Broomfield-Hinks is a Senior Account Executive at Amazon Web Services. In 2020 I conducted some virtual training for the team at Amazon and Emma was a participant. We used the Amazon 14 Leadership Principles as a basis for the stories. One of those principles was 'ownership'.

The official definition of ownership provided by Amazon is:

> *Leaders are owners. They think long term and don't sacrifice long-term value for short-term results. They act on behalf of the entire company, beyond just their own team. They never say 'that's not my job'.*

Here is the story Emma shared to communicate what ownership means to her.

> *When I was six, my brother and I begged and begged my parents for a pet.*
>
> *After many months, they eventually gave in, and my brother and I became the proud owners of Cough and Tink, two goldfish. I had a cold at the time and having just learnt the word, I thought that 'Cough' would make an excellent name for a fish.*
>
> *Our parents allowed us the fish on the condition that we took full responsibility of caring for them, which meant daily feeding and cleaning out their bowl when it got dirty.*
>
> *I was always very good at feeding the fish, which was when they were at their most interactive and playful. However, as time went on, I became more lax with the cleaning side. The cleaning was much less*

fun, being rather cold and wet, but there was also the constant fear of dropping the slippery fish you were trying to manhandle from the dirty bowl to the clean one.

When I was eight, over the course of a few days I noticed that the water was getting cloudier and cloudier again and I thought to myself, 'I must remember to clean the fish bowl.' I kept putting it off for a couple of days ... and, if I'm honest with myself, I was likely hoping that someone else would do it for me.

One morning I came downstairs and headed to the bowl to feed Cough.[1] To my horror, I saw that Cough was lying on the top of the water with his eyes staring blankly and his gills unmoving.

This was the beloved pet that I had begged and begged for who was now dead because of me. My eight-year-old heart broke and I began screaming for my mum and dad and helplessly crying, knowing what I had done.

My dad came running downstairs and after seeing the fish, he sadly confirmed that Cough had passed away. At this point I was inconsolable. Despite this, he took Cough onto the sideboard and started massaging his stomach and tried putting him upright in the water and pushing him forward to get the water in his gills again.

Tears were streaming down my face but I couldn't believe it when I started to see Cough slowly revive in front of me. My dad was an absolute hero!

In all my little life up until that point I can never remember being so grateful but also feeling so responsible for something that I had caused, which could have been easily remedied had I been more responsible.

I'm sharing this with you because it reminds me of one of our leadership principles: ownership.

As a child, I easily committed to the hard work of having a pet but only really wanted to focus on the more enjoyable aspects. I hadn't really

---

[1] Unfortunately, Tink had already passed away by this point – not due to the cleaning or lack thereof but, as my brother alleged, apparently Cough bullied Tink (as fish sometimes can do).

considered the chores that would be involved, which, being neglected, almost led to his untimely end. Therefore to me, ownership is not just about the fun stuff that you want to own and be responsible for, but also the not-so-fun stuff, the stuff that is hard work and the stuff that sometimes, you really don't want to do.

At Amazon, hopefully the level of ownership you take does not result in a life-or-death outcome! But it will only be a matter of time until you will have to take ownership; this could be ownership of a process, a project or some sort of deliverable where customers or colleagues are counting on you. When you agree to own a project, I urge you to always consider and take full ownership of that project ... the good and the bad, to the best of your ability.

And just to make the happy ending even happier, Cough the fish actually went on to live for another 12 years and I think it probably makes my dad the only person to have performed CPR on a goldfish.

See the difference? This story creates connection and engagement, way more than just telling someone what the dictionary says ownership is.

Let's have a look at another example.

Be courageous and do what matters

Natalie Mina, who I first met when she was the Chief of Staff at Accenture, recently invited me to train some of the leaders at BAI Communications to help them communicate their company values through personal stories.

One of the company's values is 'Be courageous. Do what matters'. I want to share two very different stories that they use to communicate this value.

Little boy lost in the forest

This first story is from Justin Berger, the Chief Strategy Officer.

When I was just five years old my parents took me skiing for the very first time. They put me in a group lesson with nine other children all set to ski down the slope of what looked like a giant mountain to my five-year-old eyes.

I wasn't that good, despite my best efforts. It wasn't long before I started drifting from the front of the group, where I carefully listened to the instructor, to the back of the group, where I probably belonged.

As we reached a flat slope, we had to push the poles into the snow in front of us and push ourselves forward to get ahead. I found myself falling further and further behind. I saw the group move further and further away and, at some point, I suddenly couldn't see anyone anymore.

There I was, all alone in the middle of the forest on my first time on a set of skis. I started sobbing, but I kept going, pushing my poles into the snow, pushing ahead slowly. I thought 'if I just continue it will get better, I will get to the end of the slope, find the group, or find someone'. I somehow knew if I just keep going I would find a solution … I just could not give up.

After what seemed like hours — but wasn't — another group from the ski school found me and took me back to my team. I was so relieved that I felt elated.

I'm sharing this with you because to this day I'm still impressed by the determination and courage I had as a five-year-old. Despite my fear and helplessness, I persisted.

These days, every time I'm facing a hopeless and difficult situation, and I feel like I want to give up, I remind myself to be as brave and courageous as the little boy in the forest and carry on until I find the solution I'm looking for. This also reminds me of our value of 'Be courageous. Do what matters', which I've been trying to live by since I was five years old and I invite you to give it a try.

The U-turn

This next one is from Gabrielle Hall, Group Manager, Marketing.

Ten years ago, when I was playing local competition netball (which I still do today), one particular game became quite aggressive on both sides, and our team was losing. We didn't agree with the umpire's calls, which felt like they were all going one way: against us. When the umpire called me up for a reason I felt was in her imagination, I had the urge to share my feelings ... 'Where did you get your badge from?!' I asked her sarcastically. I instantly regretted it. I was angry, but I shouldn't have been so rude.

As I headed home, I reflected on the game, thinking that this isn't what I stand for. I did a U-turn and drove back to the courts. The umpire was still there, packing up. I could've taken the easy way out and said, 'I wanted to know where you got your badge, because I want to be an umpire too.' But I drew on my courage instead and apologised.

She looked at me in disbelief and told me that she had seen her fair share of animosity in her time as an umpire ... but few acts of compassion and remorse. She said that my return trip and apology had made her day.

Thank goodness I went back. If I hadn't, what right would I have to expect anyone to be respectful or accountable for their actions? I feel this more deeply now as I watch my three-year-old son and teach him those very lessons.

In both of these stories, each leader has a slightly different interpretation and experience of what 'Be courageous. Do what matters' means to them, and that is perfectly fine. Values will mean slightly different things to different people. As long as that interpretation is consistent with what is intended, then it's okay to share the story. In fact, it's ideal, since, without their own interpretation, they will never have that personal connection to the company value, and that is what we need for real employee engagement.

Living the values stories

Stories about employees living the values at work are powerful when it comes to encouraging the desired culture of an organisation. These stories show other employees what is expected.

Take, for example, Bendigo and Adelaide Bank. They had invested in storytelling education for the senior leaders across their three main locations of Bendigo, Adelaide and Melbourne.

They then initiated what they called 'spotlight moments'. I spoke to Head of Culture Engagement Diana 'Dee' Monaghan to find out more.

Dee advised me that while the bank still had their stated values, they had also 'identified four critical few behaviours they would need to focus on as a company to accelerate the bank's strategy'. The spotlight moments were designed to 'shine a light on employees demonstrating these behaviours'.

These behaviours were:

- Act commercially.

- Move fast to help customers achieve their goals.

- Recognise people for their impact.

- Actively challenge the status quo.

The first stage of this process was to inform and educate employees around the critical few behaviours. This was done via facilitated conversations around why culture was important and what the 'critical few behaviours' meant. As part of this process employees would talk about what behaviours they would find easy and which ones would be a challenge.

They also learned the process of how to shine a light on these behaviours, which initially started with them sharing their stories with other colleagues on Yammer. This started the process of finding these stories.

The second stage was to start sharing these stories more broadly. Some would then be written up in an article and published on their internal news channels that went to all employees. Here are two of these stories.

Living through livestock restrictions

Michael Curtis is a Bendigo-based agricultural analyst who first joined Bendigo and Adelaide Bank as a graduate in 2015. He and his team provide a range of valuable insights to customers—from industry trends and farmland values to trade imports and exports.

As spring of 2020 approached, Michael knew it was a really important time for sheep farmers to sell lamb. But this year was different.

COVID-19 restrictions were already affecting farmers and would continue to pose a problem.

Michael immediately went to his sources to look at what the data on production levels and pricing told him. He 'wanted to quantify how big the issue was going to be for our sheep farming customers'. What he found was that instead of the production increasing to the levels normally seen at this time of year, the restrictions on meat processing would keep it flat.

With the COVID-19 situation changing rapidly, Michael knew the restrictions would be causing heightened anxiety for the sheep farmers and their customers. He knew he needed to understand what this meant for the farmers at a deeper level. Michael set about answering the question, 'What does this mean for a farmer who would want to sell lamb in the coming weeks?' He also wanted to provide timeline insights to the relationship managers so they could understand what their customers would be facing in the coming weeks.

In line with our value of 'Move fast to help our customers achieve their goals', Michael did just that. Within a week he had analysed the data and communicated these valuable insights to the relationship managers to allow them to have much more relevant, effective and empathetic conversations with our customers.

Stepping up and out in Hobart

Karen Tims is a Hobart-based middle market officer at Bendigo and Adelaide Bank. Building strong customer relationships is a big part of her role, which is focused on identifying and supporting growth opportunities for her business customers.

Karen was working alongside her colleague Brent when she came across a prospective customer who she knew would benefit from our service offering. Karen's manager was on leave at that time but, instead of waiting for him to return, she and Brent decided to go and visit the customer themselves …

During the discussion, they listened to the customer's needs by drawing on the skills they had learned in my 'Customer Centred Conversation' *training. Karen was able to support the customer with their lending application. Karen said with pride that 'They were so impressed with my help that they decided to bring across all their transactional banking to us, representing more than $1.5 million of new business for our bank.'*

On a separate occasion, Karen also learned of an existing customer — a solicitor — who felt limited by their banking relationship with us. Karen immediately went to talk to the customer. Karen said, 'Knowing that solicitors' accounts can be tricky at the best of times. I wanted to help the customer navigate through the complexities of our due diligence obligations.' This involved an extensive, but necessary, data collection, identity verification and documentation process to meet anti-money laundering and counter-terrorism financing requirements. As a result of Karen's intervention, the customer provided our bank with $10 million in term deposits as well as the opportunity to tender for all their business — up to $20 million.

Karen's actions are great examples of how 'moving fast for our customers' can have a huge impact on our business and the customers we support. By putting the customer at the heart of a conversation we can make a great difference in the service we provide, while supporting our bottom line.

Short and sweet

Stories of employees living the values don't have to be long. Alan Joyce, the CEO of Qantas, often uses stories to communicate a point and because of that I often read his 'Letter from the CEO' in the Qantas magazine when I fly.

In one edition, I came across the following paragraph that very succinctly shared three stories. His letter revolved around what he loves about being CEO of Qantas and it was based on the stories he has been told about Qantas employees who have gone above and beyond. He writes:

Like the cabin crew member who, without being asked, paid special attention to a passenger with a broken wrist, right down to opening a bag of pretzels before handing them to her. Or the two engineers in Alice Springs, who had finished for the night but headed back to the airport, just in case, as soon as they heard that one of our international flights was diverting there because of a sick passenger. And the off-duty airport manager who, after disembarking a flight, noticed that a fellow passenger, waiting for his luggage, appeared to be distressed. When he learned that the passenger had misplaced his laptop on board, he took him back to the aircraft to help locate it.

This is another great example of stories about everyday interactions that can help create a connection and brand loyalty with individual customers. Sharing these stories externally in the Qantas magazine means that instead of a handful of people experiencing this customer service, many more do too. And considering Qantas usually[2] have millions of customers flying on their planes each month, that is a lot of people reading these stories!

Check and reflect

- Have you provided the environment for your employees to connect with what the company purpose, values or behaviours mean to them personally?

- Could they all share a personal story on each of the desired behaviours, values and purpose?

- Do all employees understand and connect with the company's purpose and values or are they only words on a wall?

- Do you have a process to actively find stories of employees living the values?

- If so, how widely do you share those stories? Who knows about them? Do you share them internally as well as externally?

---

[2] When there is not a global pandemic going on, that is.

CUSTOMER STORIES
SHOWCASE YOUR IMPACT
IN THE REAL WORLD

Erica Keswin wrote a *Harvard Business Review* article titled 'Use Stories from Customers to Highlight Your Company's Purpose'. One such story is of a loyal customer, recently recovering from cancer, who visited her favourite Sweetgreen location in Washington, DC. (Sweetgreen is a fast-casual healthy food chain restaurant.) The team member behind the register recognised her and mentioned that he hadn't seen her in a while. He told her she looked great, remembered her favourite salad order, and gave it to her on the house. The woman was so moved by this kindness that she wrote Sweetgreen a letter telling them how much this personalised attention meant to her. This story made the rounds through the Sweetgreen community, strengthening the company's core values and empowering team members to live them.

As Sweetgreen co-founder Nate Ru states in the article, 'Stories are the way humans exchange concepts and ideas. We want to create intimacy as we scale, and stories are the key, [so] we empower everyone to collect, on a day-to-day and weekly basis, stories of people living core values.'

Sharing stories about what your customers have experienced will strengthen your brand and amplify your impact.

Let's look at some more customer stories to unpack this in more detail.

Sweeten the deal

As the previous chapter shows, personal stories of employees acting in accordance with your company values are powerful ways to communicate your brand. Sometimes the actions of an employee delivering exceptional values have a direct and immediate impact on the customer, as the story about Sweetgreen shows.

Two of Sweetgreen's core values are

- **Add the sweet touch** — create meaningful connections every day.

- **Make an impact** — leave people better than you found them.

That act by one employee affected the customer so much that it deserves to be shared externally with a wider audience.

It is this that will create brand loyalty with existing customers, but also attract new customers. In addition, sharing the story *internally* shows other employees exactly how to 'add the sweet touch' and 'make an impact'. Nordstrom were famous for this. They would share stories of great customer service to show other employees what was expected.

Amplify their voice

Sharing customer stories also throws a spotlight on what you are achieving as a company or organisation as a whole.

One organisation that does this really well is the Obama Foundation. The Obama Foundation runs leadership programs across the globe and highlights the stories of their participants. While they would never refer to their participants as customers,[1] the concept of highlighting what they do through stories is the same.

In 2019, I was more than a tad delighted to be asked by the Obama Foundation to run storytelling training as part of the Obama Foundation Asia–Pacific leadership program. This was a 12-month program that

---

[1] They didn't call them clients, students or participants; they called them leaders.

brought together 200 emerging leaders from 33 nations and territories across the Asia–Pacific region. In December 2019 we gathered in Kuala Lumpur, Malaysia, for five days to start the program.

There were speakers from around the region, plus a session with Michelle Obama and actress Julia Roberts, as well as a session with Barack Obama and his sister Maya Soetoro-Ng.[2]

Besides the fact they had brought me in to teach the 200 leaders storytelling, I also saw their commitment to storytelling when it came to highlighting their leaders. Throughout the five days they showed a selection of videos that shared the leaders' stories of what they were achieving.

One was about Julian Aguon, a human rights lawyer from Guam. Julian held a special place in my heart because every day after the training he came up and hugged me and told me how much he loved my training sessions.

At the age of 28 Julian founded his own law firm, Blue Ocean Law, which specialises in human rights, environmental justice and protecting the rights of Indigenous peoples in the Pacific region. At the time I met him, he was working with the Pacific Network on Globalisation to ensure protection of Indigenous rights as the emergent deep-sea mining industry lays claims throughout Melanesia — in Fiji, Papua New Guinea, Tonga and Vanuatu. This story was featured as a short video that was shown at the leadership program in Malaysia and can also be found externally on the Obama Foundation website.

Julian said 'the story has done some heavy lifting' for his firm, which is the only human rights practice in the region run by an Indigenous islander. Being profiled by the Obama Foundation and shared on its wide-reaching platforms did a lot to amplify not only Julian's voice, particularly his bottom-up approach to the practice of law, but also the voices of the Indigenous communities he works with.

Since the video's release, Julian's firm has seen an increase in engagement, particularly from parties in the Asia–Pacific interested in the human rights implications not only of deep-sea mining but climate change as well.

---

[2] You can view these sessions and the videos I mention in the coming pages here: https://www.obama.org/asia-pacific-19/

During the coronavirus pandemic the Obama Foundation ramped up their focus on storytelling by featuring stories of hope, showing how some of the leaders were responding to the challenges,[3] such as Gigih Septianto in Indonesia, who turned his office space into a warehouse to source and deliver medical supplies across the country. Or Rashvin Pal Singh in Malaysia, who created open-source design files that people around the world could use to make their own face masks.

Engage and excite

Crystal Prior is the Communications Manager for the Entrepreneurs' Programme at the Department of Industry for the Australian Government. This program helps small to medium businesses achieve their goals by giving them access to expert advice and financial support through grants.

'Customer stories are a big part of how we communicate the benefits of the program,' explained Crystal.

When Crystal first joined the Entrepreneurs' Programme, they used to produce case studies on their customers. These case studies were very detailed and explained what they had done on the program, what they had achieved and how the program had helped them as individuals. While these provided some data and information, they weren't really engaging, as they lacked the human element. Also, these case studies were purely written as a report to internal stakeholders and not shared beyond that.

Crystal changed the approach to the case studies; rather than being heavy with facts and process, they would be more engaging. She even hired a journalist to help do this. The purpose was threefold. To:

1. inspire other small businesses with what was possible

2. showcase the great work some of their customers were achieving and in doing so provide them with more publicity

3. demonstrate to the senior decision makers the impact the program was making.

---

[3] All these stories, captured in video, can be seen on Obama Foundation website.

THESE THREE REASONS ARE WHY SHARING CUSTOMERS' STORIES ARE SO IMPORTANT — AND EVEN IF YOU ARE DOING IT FOR ONLY ONE OF THESE REASONS, THE OTHER TWO WILL HAPPEN AS A DEFAULT.

Crystal said they have a variety of versions for each story, depending on the audience, and they use multiple platforms to share the stories. For example, the stories are always written, but some of them are then turned into a podcast, where the individuals involved are interviewed. Stories are shared internally and some make it into the annual report. They are also communicated to other customers through social media sites.

A good example is this story about Kay Saarinen and Jo Lane, two women on the Far South Coast of New South Wales, who collaborated after the devastation caused by the Black Summer bushfires over 2019 and 2020 in Australia.

They were interviewed as part of the program's Showcase Podcast series, which is accessible via the Entrepreneurs' Programme website, and this written story also features on the website.

If resilience is driven by experiencing an extreme or unexpected event, two businesswomen from the NSW South Coast are pretty sure surviving the Black Summer Bushfires means they'll be able to handle anything the universe throws at them in the future.

After all, there's nothing like facing the full fiery fury of Mother Nature to jolt you back to what matters most, or turn your head to an entire new way of thinking.

In the months following January 2020, Kay Saarinen and Jo Lane have watched their businesses, both within the wellness space, experience interesting parallels as the aftermath of the fires forced them to stand still and decide exactly where they want to be.

The Entrepreneurs' Programme has been quick to respond, launching its Strengthening Business service to help rebuild and reboot small to medium businesses in fire-affected regions.

Just days after the South Coast re-opened its roads, experienced business facilitator Monique Donaldson travelled to meet with both Kay and Jo, and help them sort through the avalanche of assistance that tends to follow such a huge event.

So, where do you start to strengthen a business that's been impacted on so many levels?

For Kay Saarinen, her company Saarinen Organics has been happily building an enviable reputation for sustainable skincare products, using organic ingredients grown on her own farm in Wyndham, one of the worst-impacted fire zones. She readily admits she had always relied on local markets, pop-up shops and a very basic website to service her customers. But when the smoke cleared, quite literally, Kay realised she needed to ramp up the digital side of her business.

'For a few weeks there, we were fighting bushfires and were evacuated on seven separate occasions,' says Kay. 'I'd managed to get a tiny amount of space on the Instagram sites "Buy from the bush" and "Spend with them", and when we finally got into Bega to check emails, we had 50 orders waiting! It basically helped save our business.'

Kay still loves the face-to-face element of her work, but there's definitely a much stronger digital focus now. 'I'm still very much stuck on the farm, removing dead trees and fixing fences, but the digital platforms allow me to still make an income. We're actually looking at our business model in a whole new way.'

Jo Lane runs Sea Health Products, which turns wild-harvested Golden Kelp into nutraceuticals, from shampoo to seasonings. She's used the enforced downtime to reassess and start planning for her own kelp farm, which she hopes to have operational by late 2020. Jo says the fires and then COVID-19 has sharpened her business vision.

'Having the support of the Entrepreneurs' Programme and the Bega Valley Innovation Hub, as well as talking to other local business owners like Kay, you find reassurance and feel more confident, and you really feel like, "I can do this"!'

Growth facilitator Monique Donaldson says it's taken time and patience to help businesses navigate the right financial support, but many have been just as appreciative of having someone who can see beyond the hardship for new opportunities.

'Kay's business is now looking to make connections and upscale the production of her Saarinen Organics, including a new factory, while Jo wants to collaborate more with researchers, and we've linked her into the CSIRO to help with planning for her new kelp farm,' says Monique.

What I like about this story is that Kay and Jo are the focus of the story; they are the heroes. There are only subtle messages at the end about the program itself. This story also appeared in the annual report and in that version, the focus shifted more to the program and the benefits for that publication.

It's a really good example of the importance of changing the focus of the story depending on the audience.

I spoke to Kay and Jo to ask them how the Entrepreneurs' Programme sharing their story has helped them. Kay advised that 'they have been fantastic getting our story out there on all their social media platforms'. The sharing of their story has significantly increased their exposure, resulting in a long-form story for the TV news show *The Project*.

Jo also echoed the benefits of the exposure, in sales but predominantly in increased opportunities to work alongside other organisations on sustainability, such as the Commonwealth Scientific and Industrial Research Organisation (CSIRO) and Wollongong University.

Jo added, 'Sharing of that story has meant more people want to speak to us to share the story again. And every time I have this opportunity to tell my story, I reconnect with the purpose of why I started this.' She says that 'it is very easy to get stuck in the day-to-day tasks of operating a business, but sharing my story reinvigorates me again and again'.

Finding the right stories

There is a lot of investment in finding and sharing these types of stories, so it is important that the selected stories have the greatest impact to ensure the best return on investment. Crystal and the team are responsible for collecting what they call 'story leads'. Crystal decides which stories are more valuable than others by using defined criteria.

Crystal says 'it's not about customers just making lots of money'. Rather, they look for customers that have:

- made an impact and a difference in their community

- done something quite innovative to achieve their goals

- done something very unusual

- had a very interesting outcome.

Crystal believes when a story meets at least one or two of the above criteria, they are more interesting for a consumer to read and also can better show other customers what is achievable. For example, the story of Medalfield CEO Dan Hannigan, who grew up in Far North Queensland near a landfill dump and is now working with James Cook University to use microwave technology to break down plastics. Or Hatch Biosystems founder Claire Leach, who is showing how her unique flock of black soldier flies holds the key to diverting thousands of tonnes of food waste from landfill every year.

Check and reflect

- What interesting case studies do you have that you could turn into more engaging case stories?

- Do you have some positive customer feedback that you could share internally to encourage more of that behaviour?

- What stories could you share (as well as the facts) to help with ongoing funding of a project?

- How have your products or services benefited your customers, and can you share stories about that?

- Do you have a process for finding these customer stories?

- Could you share your customers' stories to help amplify their voice?

CHALLENGE STORIES
TALES OF WHEN THE GOING GETS TOUGH

In November 2014, after a year of significant growth in my business, my husband decided to leave his senior corporate role. In the same week, my friend Elise accepted my offer to leave her career as a primary school teacher and come and work with me, full-time, as my executive manager. Even though this had been discussed for a couple of months, when they both made their respective decisions, I felt the weight of responsibility terrifying. At one point, I remember feeling like I was going to vomit. It was now up to me to continue the success I had experienced over the last 12 months, to keep Elise employed, and, as the only breadwinner, to keep ... well, bread (and other things) on the table.

It's a story that I often share when I'm being interviewed and asked about times of self-doubt or challenges. I also share it when I'm mentoring people on the ups and downs of running your own business.

There are often many challenges in business, especially in the early days of struggles, setbacks and self-doubts. These can all be very powerful stories, yet they are often not shared because they involve us showing vulnerability.

Through the amazing work of Brené Brown, however, we have come to realise that showing vulnerability is not a sign of weakness, but rather a sign of strength and courage.[1]

WHEN HAVE YOU BEEN CHALLENGED AND WHAT DID YOU DO TO OVERCOME IT?

Personal challenges

A good example of a challenge story comes from the founder of Mekong Capital, Chris Freund. (A case story features him later in the book.) When I first heard this story, it had a great impact on me. It's a story that Chris shares often; this is an edited version of what is also on the Mekong Capital website.

In early 2008, I had just begun the journey to become the leader that would hopefully cause Mekong Capital to dramatically improve its performance and achieve its full potential. Running a business like Mekong Capital had turned out to be much more difficult than I expected when I founded the firm back in 2001. I had a lot of doubts about myself and my ability to lead the team. For example, I would have thoughts like: I don't understand Vietnamese people, they are too short-term; they refuse to accept my leadership; our team keeps choosing to be polarised with 'us vs them' thinking and I don't know how to get everyone aligned around common goals; I am not a people person; I am all alone here; I wish someone else would step up to provide some leadership; etc.

Mekong Capital had engaged a consulting company, a subsidiary of Landmark Education, to help us transform our corporate culture. The head of Landmark in Asia was a man named Jerome Downes, who had been leading these programs since the mid-70s, when it was known as EST. Jerome was committed to causing people to be transformed and empowered, and he had a personal goal to cause millions of people in Asia to transform. To me Jerome was a true master, and I felt like I was a struggling apprentice. Jerome had made a commitment to me

---

[1] Brené Brown also said one of my favourite story-related quotes: 'Maybe stories are just data with a soul.'

to help us create a new future for Mekong Capital, and to enable us to transform our whole organisation.

Our corporate culture transformation initially faced a lot of internal resistance. Suddenly we were holding people accountable and expecting them to be responsible to deliver clearly stated results rather than tolerating excuses. This is something we hadn't been doing before and many employees didn't like that — some people wanted to be right about the excuses and explanations they had been making, and not suddenly held accountable for results. There was a lot of employee turnover and a lot of complaints about what was wrong with me, or wrong with the senior management of Mekong Capital. Employees and our investors were constantly challenging us on why we were spending so much time and money to transform our culture. I was committed to see this through, but also feeling very surprised and frustrated by all of the resistance, and didn't know how to get our team to start choosing to take individual responsibility rather than blaming others. I would think: Why couldn't everyone just do what's best for the company and get aligned around our goals? What is wrong with this company?

Often I found myself being a victim of the situation that initially very few other people in Mekong had taken a strong stand for this transformation. I was waiting and hoping for some other team members to step up and take a strong stand for this transformation process, and feeling disappointed when they didn't. I wanted other people to share the burden of leadership with me, and I felt all alone.

It was times like these when I was being unsure of my ability to lead, and feeling like a victim of others, that Jerome would communicate to me that he had the full expectation that I would step in to provide leadership, take a stand for what the future of Mekong Capital looks like, and that I would enrol others into my vision. Jerome spoke to me as if it was not the true me to be a victim of the idea that employees weren't yet stepping up to provide leadership, or weren't yet aligning around the future that I saw. As a result of his coaching, I saw that our employees won't provide leadership until I provide leadership, and that it all starts with me and who I am being. I realised: If I'm blaming them, they will be blaming someone as well. If I take full responsibility, some of them will start to take responsibility as well.

So I started to be responsible to get our team members' alignment by having one-on-one direct conversations with specific team members, and not avoiding any uncomfortable topics, until they were either on board or not on board. Some people weren't the right fit and chose to resign. But as time passed, more and more of our team members were choosing to provide leadership and really embrace our transformation and our new culture, and the new people that were joining were a strong cultural fit.

While I was struggling through this, we were working towards aligning on our first company vision for Mekong Capital. In November 2009, a few weeks before our vision was completed, Jerome learned that he had a serious heart problem and would need surgery in Thailand. Jerome delayed his surgery by three weeks in order to assist us to complete our vision because he had committed to us that we would complete it. Sadly, there was a complication during his surgery and he passed away shortly after on 25 December 2009. It was such a sad loss, and happened so much sooner than I was ready, and I couldn't stop crying for days. But it was now time for me to fully stand on my own as the leader of Mekong Capital, and Jerome had full faith in me that I could do it.

Since that time, Jerome has always been my inspiration for what it looks like to be a leader, to see the best in people and hold people accountable to achieve their full potential. He saw something in me that was bigger than what I saw in myself.

In his memory, we named one of our core values after him. The core value Jeromosity means 'Relating to other people as their commitments, intentions, possibilities, and inherent goodness. Empowering others.'

I'm committed to living up to what Jerome saw in me, to honour his memory by causing Mekong Capital to achieve its vision of reinventing private equity. Imagine what's possible if each of us lives up to our full potential, and holds each other accountable for doing so.

I love the vulnerability that Chris is prepared to show in this story and the courage that he has to share this in the public domain. It also shows his passion for what he does. There are so many valuable lessons in this story and it communicates effectively the type of leader Chris is and the culture that he has helped create at Mekong Capital.

Responding to a challenge

Challenge stories do not always have to be about how the founders or leaders have worked through internal challenges. They could also be stories about how the company has responded to an external challenge; for example, this story about Transpower New Zealand.

Transpower is the national electricity provider for New Zealand. In December 2017 they encountered a major outage in Northland. This was due to vandals shooting bullets into three towers, and it was not expected that they would have power restored for 48 hours. However, they managed to work together to get power back in less than a day.

They were so proud of the employees and partners involved, they made a short video of the event highlighting the efforts of the people involved in the restoration of the power that day. This video is still shared widely, both internally and externally, to demonstrate what can be achieved, even in the face of seemingly insurmountable odds, when teams come together to work towards a common goal.

Other really great challenge stories have surfaced as a result of the coronavirus.

Anyone up for a drink?

When the demand for hand sanitiser far outweighed the supply, Sydney-based distillery Archie Rose swapped production to produce hand sanitiser.

This is a story that features on their website.

> Since March 23 Archie Rose Distilling Co. has switched its production focus to produce 101 959 x 500ml equivalent bottles of Hand Sanitiser to date in an effort to bolster national supplies and enable

the redeployment of its fifteen-strong bar team as well as create new employment for an additional twelve hospitality workers.

Prompted by the government's full bar shutdown on 20 March, Archie Rose immediately re-prioritised its manufacturing focus from whisky, gin and vodka production to hand sanitiser, releasing its first batch on 23 March and four other batches since — with the distillery now intending to manufacture the product for as long as is required.

Each release has met with unprecedented demand from the general public, government bodies and essential services along with a range of large and small hospitality and retail businesses, including Endeavour Drinks and 2250 units to independent bars, restaurants and bottle shops.

The story goes on to include quotes from the company's founder Will Edwards.

It's been one hell of an effort and many long days and nights, but as we already possessed the required federal licences, dangerous goods approvals, access to raw materials and expertise, the switch from whisky, gin and vodka to neutral ethanol and hand sanitiser was a tough but clear call. To be able to assist with bolstering national supplies while securing the employment of our previously stood down bar team, and now to offer work to an additional twelve hospitality staff who had lost their jobs due to COVID-19 is unbelievable, and a massive morale boost to our whole team who have worked so hard to make it happen.

Securing a steady volume of packaging to support the production switch has been incredibly difficult, as has adapting our warehouse to meet the demands of packing and shipping an unprecedented number of unique products that differ in format to our usual spirits. We're really thankful for the support we've received from suppliers, customers and the government, and for people's patience as we've navigated the transition from being a spirits and hospitality business to producing hundreds of thousands of bottles of hand sanitiser.

I spoke to their head of marketing, Victoria Tulloch, about the impact this has had on their brand. Victoria took me back to Friday 20 March 2020, when the government mandated the closure of all restaurants and bars.

Archie Rose have a bar at their distillery and she said this decision to close bars meant that their 15 bar staff would potentially lose their jobs.

That, combined with the national shortage of hand sanitiser, resulted in them making an almost immediate decision that they would switch production from spirits to hand sanitiser. This meant that they were one of the first distilleries to do this. And when I say immediate, I mean immediate. Within three days they had sourced bottles for the hand sanitisers, reconfigured their production line, created and printed labels, amended their insurance policies, and obtained additional federal production licences, plus they were abiding by all the legal and health requirements for the hand sanitisers and coronavirus work restrictions, to produce 7500 units … in just three days.

The story had an instant connection. Victoria told me they were featured well over 50 times in press articles, TV and radio around the world, including Japanese TV and BBC radio.

This exposure was not the reason they did it, but, as Victoria said, it was 'a welcomed yet unexpected by-product'. Victoria advised me that they have a very strong connection to their company values that drives their decisions, two of their values being innovation and quality. Because these values are so embedded in the way they work, they knew they could innovate quickly and to such a high standard.

They went on to produce 120 000 units until the supply had met demand before they reverted to producing spirits. They also created 30 jobs, meaning that their current 15 bar staff were continuing to be employed, along with another 15 locals they hired who had lost their jobs to the coronavirus restrictions affecting the hospitality industry.

The positive impact to their brand has been outstanding. Victoria advised that within four months of the story spreading about their hand sanitiser, they doubled their database from 50 000 to 100 000 contacts. Their social media platform grew by 30 per cent, and she believes that their brand awareness was accelerated by at least 12 to 18 months.

For a young brand this is a major win. I would also suggest they have generated some pretty strong employee engagement and loyalty along the way.

**SHOWING HOW YOU CAN RESPOND TO A CHALLENGE
FOR ALL THE RIGHT REASONS IS A STORY
THAT NOT ONLY CUSTOMERS WILL CONNECT WITH,
BUT ALSO EMPLOYEES.**

Hotel of hope

Along with hospitality, tourism was another massively affected industry in 2020. All hotels were affected by travel bans as they responded to the COVID-19 challenge. This email from Arne Sorenson, Marriott International President and CEO, went out to all customers.

Marriott understands that the pulse of the world beats as one to overcome COVID-19 and its devastating impact around the globe. As we all watch the news unfold about this unprecedented event, it's clear that there is a need to assist and bolster healthcare workers and community caregivers who are on the frontlines working to contain this disease. To that end, we have established the following programs to aid in the urgent fight against the pandemic.

Around the world, our hotels located in close proximity to hospitals are in a unique position to help. Many of these properties are providing respite to weary hospital workers, military personnel and supermarket employees who need to stay close to work or are concerned about going home to their loved ones. In Suzhou, China, associates at five Marriott brand hotels found another way to help first responders. When a local surgical mask factory announced that it needed workers, about 30 of our associates volunteered to help manufacture and package the masks. The work was physically taxing but with their help and the help of others, the factory began producing 100 000 masks per day. It's that kind of spirit that will sustain us through this crisis.

Given the unprecedented disruption to the travel industry, a number of our hotels have, unfortunately, had to close temporarily. Even as the hotels were shutting their doors, associates from New Delhi, India, to Santos, Brazil, have found multiple ways to support the communities in which the hotels are located. The Riviera Marriott Hotel La Porte de Monaco and AC Hotel Nice, for example, donated all of their unused produce and food products to a local children's charity, which provides housing and other services for endangered children. Many of our properties have contributed by providing food, pre-packed and cooked meals to crisis relief efforts and much-needed supplies like cleaning products, masks, gloves, anti-microbial wipes, sanitisers and shower caps for medical and other frontline workers. And in a beautiful sign of solidarity among us all, many of our teams have illuminated their hotel windows with symbols of love and messages of hope.

Hearing these stories creates a magnetic attraction. Will it make me instantly book a Marriott hotel? Not necessarily. But it will certainly make me consider them when I next book a hotel.

All companies will go through challenges, either internal or external, and they all respond in a different way. The challenges may be significant or minor.

IT WAS WINSTON CHURCHILL WHO SAID 'NEVER LET A GOOD CRISIS GO TO WASTE', SO IF YOU'VE HAD ONE, IT'S WORTH THINKING OF WHAT STORIES YOU COULD SHARE ABOUT IT.

Check and reflect

- What challenges has your company had to overcome, and is there a story there that is worth sharing?

- If you are the founder or current CEO, what challenges have you personally had to overcome, and are they worth sharing?

- Was there a time when your values were tested, and is that a story worth sharing?

- Do you have any challenge stories from the coronavirus that would be worth recording and sharing?

- Could you highlight your employees who are responding to challenges, either their own or in their community?

COMMUNITY STORIES
BRINGING LIFE TO CORPORATE RESPONSIBILITY

Remember the creation story I shared of Who Gives A Crap earlier? Well I first heard about this company when my elder daughter, Alex, was on my case to buy their toilet paper because they were an ethical business. It was not that I disagreed with her, but it was during a time when I felt that every single purchasing decision I made was being judged, criticised and debated by my daughters.[1]

Fast forward to the start of the worldwide coronavirus epidemic and there was panic buying of toilet paper ... one of the most ridiculous examples of human behaviour. I received this message from Danny Alexander, who is based in New York and one of the co-founders of Who Gives A Crap.

Hey there,

Danny here, one of the co-founders of Who Gives A Crap. What times we're living in, huh? I'm wearing slippers and writing from my dining room table, which is now my office. My wife is on the couch (which is now her office), and my dog is snoring at my feet. We've got water boiling on the stove for tea, and the kittens we're fostering are tumbling around in the hallway. It's not our usual office setup, but it works.

---

[1] To tell you the truth it was doing my head in and I was more than a bit over it, so I just ignored them.

This also isn't the usual email we send. There's nothing fancy here. This is just me, writing to you, to share some things that I hope might make you feel a bit better. The air has been heavy with bad news recently, but so many good things have emerged as well. We want to share them with you.

It followed with an acknowledgement that they were benefiting from the panic buying of toilet paper.

You've probably heard it's a pretty good time to be in the toilet paper business, and it is. Even though we sold out in early March, it was still our biggest month in history, and we hope the next few months will be big as well.

The email then went on to explain that they are making an 'immediate $100 000 AUD donation to four of our charity partners that are helping the most vulnerable people deal with this global crisis'.

They also advised that in the coming weeks they would have enough toilet paper for their customers but were sending the first batches to the people who need it most. So they had 'donated 10 000 rolls of toilet paper to Foodbank Victoria, who is helping distribute household essentials to people in need near our team in Melbourne', and they were working with their people in the United States and the UK to do the same.

The email then went on to talk about what some of their employees were doing. Such as Tiger, who had been grocery shopping for the elderly in LA. Jean, who helped organise vegetable donations for families in Manila. Amy, who donated 600 bars of soap to a village in Malawi, where she used to live. And my favourite, Bruce, who volunteered to teach his partner to drive in Taiwan's empty streets, saying, 'This may not be saving the world, but it is true bravery!'

The email wasn't about their product; it was about everybody else in their community, and it ended with:

Virtual elbow bumps,

Danny (and the whole Who Gives A Crap team)

P.S. Sorry if you were expecting this to be about new toilet paper. We're still sold out, but I promise you we're working on it. If you're looking for stock updates, click here. Or you could join our waiting list here. Just want to watch a Chihuahua skateboard? Click here.

I actually read the whole email and clicked through to all the links about their employees and customers. I am now a devoted purchaser of Who Gives A Crap toilet paper. It was the stories that I connected to, which made me purchase the product.

SisterWorks

In 2020 I was asked to be ambassador for SisterWorks, which is a not-for-profit organisation that provides support for women refugees, asylum seekers and migrants. I went and met the founder, Luz Restrepo, who shared the story of how SisterWorks started. It's a story that is told to all employees, to the many audiences Luz speaks in front of, and is also on the website under 'Our Founder's Story'.

At the age of 45, as a medical doctor and a communication expert, Luz Restrepo arrived in Australia in 2010 seeking political asylum. Her life was in tatters and she spoke no English. She felt like a nobody: frightened, isolated and disempowered. Luz soon discovered that she was not alone.

In 2011, along with a group of 25 women experiencing similar challenges, Luz began to make and sell crafts around Melbourne. She understood that to support each other is also to strengthen each other.

SisterWorks Inc. was born in May 2013 when a committee of volunteers joined Luz with legal, fund-raising, marketing and administrative skills to give support and structure to the project.

While Luz is no longer CEO, she is still the founder, and so this story lives on and is still used and shared by the company. It shows how the organisation started as well as the work they do in the community.

You don't need to be a not-for-profit or ethical company to share stories about the good things you are doing in your community.

Many large organisations fulfil their corporate responsibility obligations by helping out the community with donations, grants, support programs or employee volunteer schemes.

While many communicate this on their website and annual report, they tend to focus on the stats as opposed to the stories: listing the amount of money donated, the number of people who received help, the hours of volunteer services gifted. This information is normally needed for compliance reports but it generally doesn't make for interesting reading.

Like the Entrepreneurs' Programme mentioned in the previous chapter on customer stories, organisations should also have different versions of community stories depending on the purpose of sharing and the audience.

The global professional services firm EY do such a thing by sharing stories in different formats of their employees that are making a difference in their community.

Showing Faith

One such story is about Faith Buhle Moyo from Zimbabwe. Her community story is featured on the EY website in written and video format.[2] Her story started from her own experience of being an entrepreneur in Zimbabwe and not having access to knowledge or help to sustain her small business.

Part of her story reads …

In Zimbabwe, growing a small business is an uphill battle. Entrepreneurial mentorship is not prevalent in the country, and many Zimbabweans open businesses without the proper knowledge to run a successful business. With no access to resources or management skills to overcome basic challenges, many small businesses fail within the first few months. Those that survive often have trouble accelerating their

---

[2] To watch this video, search for 'Strengthening our communities Faith Moyo' on YouTube.

growth, and tend to stagnate unless they are able to secure resources or foreign currency from angel investors or banks.

Faith Moyo experienced this firsthand when she opened up a successful coffee shop with her father. She believed her business had potential; but, like most Zimbabweans, Faith and her father lacked the business acumen or financial management skills to manage its growth. When the shop closed two years later, Faith wondered what could have been if there was a professional service organisation to help her and her father through their growth.

It goes on to say,

Now working in the EY member firm office in Zimbabwe, she's determined to help her country's entrepreneurs access the kind of professional support she and her father needed. She helped launch the EY Business Accelerator program in 2017 and currently acts as the project manager.

It then talks briefly about the program and the difference it is making before coming back to Faith and mentioning that she and her team

also spend their free time speaking to entrepreneurs about financial management at various speaking engagements. To date, they've reached more than 800 people.

Through Faith's work, Zimbabwe's next generation of entrepreneurs isn't left to figure out how to drive sustainable growth on their own. They have a passionate, dedicated and experienced resource willing to help them every step of the way.

Faith's story was also featured as one of the global winners of the EY award 'Better Begins With You'. I spoke to Faith to find out how winning the award, but, more importantly, EY sharing her story has helped her and her cause.

Faith told me that the opportunities that have come about because of the award and subsequent sharing of her story have been overwhelming. From a program perspective, Faith said it has given her 'access to all the right people'. She has had associations asking how they can support the program, and enquiries from people outside of Zimbabwe wanting to know if the program is run in other countries.

From a personal perspective she is now being asked to come and share her story around the world, from the local university in Zimbabwe to the EY American leadership program. It was during the former speech that a colleague of hers from Chicago was inspired to run the same program there.

Faith said that the most significant impact that EY sharing her story has achieved is that she has been able to reach more people and have a greater impact.

Before we ended our call, I asked her how her dad feels. She beamed with pride when she told me 'he is so proud' and 'so excited'. He was even a participant in the second cohort of the program, and he often gets recognised from the video.

The real benefit of companies sharing employees' stories of the good things they do in the community is demonstrated in the final story Faith shares with me. Soon after EY shared her story, before she'd had any public speaking experience telling her story, she received a call from a preacher who went to the same gym as her dad. The preacher asked her to come and speak to the young people at his congregation. Which she did; it was her first ever public speaking experience. She said the feedback from those young people was so inspiring, saying that 'nothing inspires me more than inspiring the youth'.

EY, in sharing her story, gave her a platform to do more of that.

While the story of Faith is also about how EY are supporting the program, not all stories about your employees helping out in the community have to be tied back to any specific company-sponsored initiative. For example, the short stories shared on the Who Gives A Crap email about their employees just helping their neighbours were incredibly effective.

HIGHLIGHTING THESE GOOD DEEDS NOT ONLY DOES WONDERS FOR YOUR EMPLOYEES' PERSONAL BRAND AND REPUTATION, BUT BY ASSOCIATION IT ALSO REFLECTS WELL ON YOUR BRAND AND REPUTATION.

Check and reflect

- Are your stories actually stories, or just a bunch of numbers and percentages?

- Could you share stories about what your company is doing to support your community (but not have it feel like advertising)?

- Do you have employees doing good things in their community and can you share those stories, regardless of whether it's related to a company-sponsored initiative or not?

- Are you using a variety of channels to share stories?

- Do you have different versions of the story depending on what channel you are using and who your audience is?

implement brand STORY telling

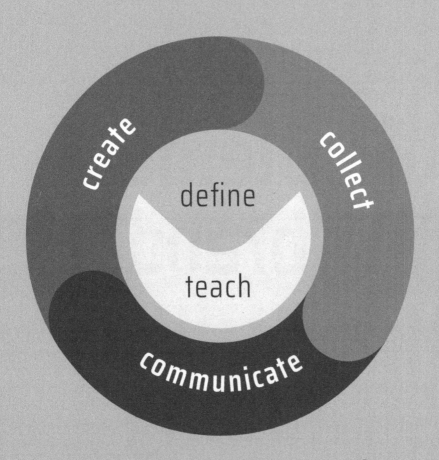

Figure 1 Implementing Brand Storytelling

Hopefully you've got some insights into the different types of stories you can share, and are inspired to actually create your own magnetic brand stories. Now, let's look at helping you implement brand storytelling.

I have been working with organisations for over a decade and a half to help them communicate more effectively through stories. For a whole lot of reasons, some have implemented storytelling better than others. Over this time, I have developed a pretty good idea on what works and what doesn't and the pitfalls to avoid.

So in the following pages I'm going to take you through my model for implementing brand storytelling in organisations. It's an approach that will help any business communicate their brand, both internally and externally. (Remember, when we are talking about brand we are talking about the culture, strategy, values, behaviours, purpose, vision and mission.) This approach is laid out in figure 1.

The elements of implementing brand storytelling are:

- **Define:** be clear on your brand. Organisations will have various names for these messages, and it is normally outlined on a strategic document detailing such things as mission, vision, purpose, values, strategic objectives, focus areas and desired behaviours.

- **Teach:** educate employees about the power of stories. This means teaching employees how to find stories and share them in a concise yet engaging way. This step is critical because it's about experiencing firsthand the magnetic power of stories. Your employees will be more capable, confident and committed when it comes to collecting, communicating and creating stories.[1]

- **Collect:** find magnetic stories to communicate your brand. It could be something that happened years ago or something that happened yesterday. It could be stories from head office or back office. It's all about collating the stories that respect the past, acknowledge the present and inspire the future.

---

[1] That is a lot of 'c' words.

- **Communicate:** share your stories to help connect and engage with people. Communicate internally and externally; in written and oral formats; on traditional media and social media; using formal channels and informal channels … and everything in between. The education process is essential to ensure employees are set up for success to do this well.

- **Create:** understand how your actions can generate stories, whether it be interactions with customers or interactions with fellow employees. If people have a positive experience they will share positive stories. Likewise, if they have a negative experience they will share that as well! Being aware of how actions can create stories is critical to make sure it all works *for* you, not against you.

Implementing brand storytelling is not finite and not sequential — although in my experience, organisations get better results when they start with defining their brand and teaching storytelling.

The cyclic nature of the model then kicks in and these stories of your brand in action can then be collected and communicated, resulting in a spiral effect of more stories being shared to reinforce your brand.

Ready?

DEFINE
KNOW WHAT YOUR
BRAND IS (AND ISN'T)

Before any company starts thinking about the stories they could share with others, they first need to be clear on what messages they want to communicate. What stories do you want people sharing about you when you are not in the room? What do you want your brand to be? (Remember, your brand is your purpose, values and behaviours.)

When I conduct brand storytelling workshops with individuals, I ask them to do some pre-work. Firstly, I ask them to think about what they want their desired brand to be. I ask them to think of five words or phrases that they would be happy with if people used these to describe them. It has to be authentic … this isn't about you pretending to be someone else. It also has to be realistic, but can include room for growth and evolution. It's not a wish list.

Once they have completed that first step, they then need to go away and actually ask five people that they have regular interactions with to list five words or phrases they would use to describe them. It's important to ask a diverse set of people that they currently deal with. It could be their manager, some of their team, co-workers, clients, or suppliers. It's also important that they ask people who will give them honest descriptors.

I then get them to compare how they'd like to be described with how they are actually described. This determines how aligned you currently are with your brand. A wide and deep variation could indicate a challenge. For example, if someone wanted to be known as strategic but none of the five people described them as strategic it would indicate that there is probably some work or change that needs to take place — which is not 'bad', it just means they will need to highlight this part more. However, if they wanted to be described as collaborative but all five described them as someone who 'works best alone', then maybe the desired brand is too far of a stretch.

This same process can be followed for organisations. Yet many organisations make it overcomplicated, bringing in external consultants and spending months to determine what their values and purpose should be, then spending even more time wordsmithing everything.

Don't get caught up on what you call them

Companies can spend a lot of time and effort (sometimes way too much) coming up with unique names for values and desired behaviours, such as our 'DNA', our 'code', the way we 'rock and roll'. In the end, it doesn't really matter what you call them.

WHAT IS IMPORTANT IS THAT YOU KNOW WHAT YOU WANT YOUR BRAND TO BE.

I recall a time when my younger daughter, Jess, was in grade 6. It was their athletics day and Jess was running in a 1.5-kilometre race competing with her classmates, as they were split into the four school houses. I asked her how she went and she informed me that she didn't go very well as she wasn't feeling great. But, not wanting to give up, she kept going and even managed to pass a few people at the end. Then she went on to say that she was really happy because two of her close friends came first and second, so there was cause for celebration even though they were competing in the other houses.

As a parent I was very proud of her: for not giving up and giving it a go, but also for being more excited about her friends' accomplishments than winning ... and I told Jess this.

To her it doesn't matter what I labelled that. Did I call it a 'value in action', a 'desired behaviour', our 'family code'? I could have called it any of those but I didn't call it anything. But she knew from my acknowledgement that it was the right thing to do. It's the type of behaviour that will not only be recognised but also expected in the future.

CALLING OUT GOOD BEHAVIOUR ENCOURAGES FUTURE GOOD BEHAVIOUR.

Your brand in three easy steps

Organisations will go through the process of defining their brand in a variety of ways. Some may undertake a long, collaborative approach, gathering as much input from employees and other stakeholders as possible, sometimes bringing in an external company to assist them. In others, a new CEO may be appointed and just make a 'captain's call' on the values.

The approach that I undertake with individuals, outlined at the start of this chapter, works just as well for companies, whether you are in a start-up or a large multinational:

- Write down five words or phrases that you want other people to describe your company as. (These words are going to define your brand.)

- Then ask other people how they would describe your company in five words or phrases. (You can include as many employees, stakeholders and customers as you like in this process.)

- Now compare them. Are they close or are they poles apart? Ideally you would want them to be relatively similar. If not, you have some work to do!

Aurecon, an engineering, design and advisory company with over 7500 employees, went through a similar process. They interviewed their clients to gain a more accurate picture of how they were currently seen by others ... what was their brand? They landed on five brand words they called 'attributes'. Now, when anyone applies for a job at Aurecon they do a quiz that determines which attribute they are most personally aligned to. The successful applicants, besides getting a job, also get a coffee mug with their attribute on it as part of their induction.

Now before you roll your eyes at the thought of another coffee mug with a value printed on it, hear me out. Danielle Bond, Group Director of Brand, Marketing and Communications at Aurecon, explains that the attribute on the coffee mug serves as a catalyst for a conversation between new employees and their colleagues. These conversations bring clarity to what the brand attributes mean for the new employee and help to keep the brand attributes visible.

Authentic and congruent

You may be thinking that this is all getting a bit too manufactured; surely if you just do what is true to you, then you will be known for that. And to some extent that is correct. If you are always a person who does what they say they will do, you will get a reputation for that. Part of your brand will be reliable. If, on the other hand, you hardly ever do what you say, you will be known as unreliable.

In business it's the same thing. If you always deliver great customer service you will become known for that. It will form part of your brand. If you are pretty slack with customer service, you will be known for that and that will become part of your brand. If you treat your employees well, over time you will be known for that and vice versa.

YOUR ACTIONS OVER TIME WILL DETERMINE YOUR BRAND.

Ideally, what you want your brand to be should be authentic and congruent to who you are. If you are trying to be something that you're not, or that doesn't come naturally to you, then it's simply pretending and not sustainable. As an individual, if you want to be known as strategic but you are a very detailed person then it might take more effort to change into that. The same with a company: if you want to be known as innovative and responsive but have cumbersome bureaucratic processes and systems and have employees resistant to change, then it's going to take a lot of work to change that.

It can be done, but you will need to be quite deliberate in how you go about changing the brand.

Deliberate versus organic

Being deliberate with your approach when it comes to brand means you can take greater control of it. You also need to be aware of how a brand can develop organically; if you're not aware of this you could lose control of your brand ... and very quickly.

Let me provide a personal example of how organic versus deliberate brand formation can work.

I left the corporate world in 2005, selling storytelling into organisations. I didn't do an overly sophisticated brand exercise, but I did know that one of the things I wanted to be known for was being professional yet different. This was aligned with the concept of storytelling. I wanted to be seen as a professional, but one who was communicating in a different way. And different in a good way, not like when you serve up a meal and people comment that it's 'different' as a polite way of saying they don't like it. So I was very deliberate when it came to communicating this, from the way I dressed (often in jeans and a blazer) to what my website looked like.

Fast forward to few years ago. I was strolling down a street in Fitzroy, Melbourne, and walked past a shoe shop that had some pretty cool-looking shoes. Now, one of the things that I have hated throughout my entire life is shopping for shoes. I never knew what worked for me, and as a female there was (and still is) this pressure to wear high heels. I think because I didn't value shoes I didn't invest a lot of money or time in buying them, so I just ended up with crappy shoes. (Seriously: I used to prefer going to the dentist to shoe shopping.)

Anyway, a pair of shoes caught my eye in this shop so I went in, tried them on, and, with encouragement from my daughter, decided to buy them. They were flat and dark green and I learned they were called brogues. They were so comfortable — not cheap (so a step up for me), but so much value for money. They were also from a local Melbourne designer (Habbot shoes), so it's always nice to support local talent.

I loved them so much I purchased another pair. These ones were flat and silver. A lot of people started to comment on my shoes. I mean a *lot*. I would walk into a lift and complete strangers would comment on them. I would be sitting in a plane and the person sitting next to me would comment, or the flight attendants. I remember walking off stage one day and someone approached me saying, 'I could not listen to what you were saying for the first few minutes because I was so captivated by your shoes.' So I kept buying the same brand of shoes, which now comprises approximately 75 per cent of my shoe collection.

Without meaning to, I was becoming known for my shoes ... and this is coming from someone who hated shoes! Because the shoes fitted with my brand of 'professional but different', I was happy for this to occur. But it happened organically; I never once thought, 'You know what would be good for my brand, is to go and find myself some professional but different shoes.' It just happened.

But then it turned deliberate. So much so that the photo of me on the cover of my previous book deliberately included a shot of me wearing these shoes ... and now I feel a bit of pressure to always wear these shoes! People seem genuinely disappointed if I turn up in an ordinary pair of shoes, so I just don't. (It's permission to keep updating my Habbot shoe collection.)

I share this as it's an example of something happening organically; but because I was aware of what I wanted my brand to be, I then made deliberate decisions to emphasise it. And it's important to note that this was about enhancing my brand, not pretending to be something that I wasn't.

To contrast this, let me share with you another example of when something happened organically, only it was not aligned to my brand so I deliberately de-emphasised it.

Over the years, my messages to my audiences about storytelling started to also emphasise the importance of real communication and being authentic to your own values and beliefs. (To the point that my previous book was titled *Real Communication: How to Be You and Lead True*.)

So I was aware that 'real' was also becoming part of my brand.

Then something happened at the start of the coronavirus pandemic. About six months earlier, for the first time I had SNS on my nails[1] (which I am positive makes you type faster).[2] When we went into lockdown restrictions and beauty salons closed, I thought it could be a fun challenge to see how far I could grow out my SNS nails before they either snapped off or I succumbed and removed them myself. I posted this on Instagram as a bit of fun. To my surprise they lasted longer than I thought. Every week I would post an update on Instagram with how many nails had succumbed and how many were still standing. I could not believe the interaction I was getting. Over the weeks people started tagging me in Instagram posts and Facebook posts about nails. All of a sudden, in a matter of weeks, fake nails[3] were starting to become my thing and part of my brand. First of all, it's not my thing: I have never really been into nail polish at all, let alone fake nails. So from a personal perspective it didn't sit well.

From a brand perspective, it was bit disturbing. As someone who wants to be known for being real, I don't want to be known for fake nails. I'm not saying I have never had SNS again — I have. But, unlike the shoes, I didn't want to emphasise this. So I just stopped posting about it on social media.

IT MAKES GOOD BUSINESS SENSE TO BE AWARE OF WHAT YOUR BRAND IS AND WHAT YOU DO TO INFLUENCE THAT.

Defining it is the first step of taking control of it. And be aware that this can happen with a very deliberate approach, but it can also happen organically, so you need to ensure everything you do is in line with your brand.

---

[1] If you're a man, ask your wife, daughters or female friends.

[2] Well, it at least sounds like it does.

[3] I know technically they are not fake. They're my nails — just with a truckload of powder and glue piled on top.

The next step to taking control of your brand is looking for the stories you can actively collect and communicate to reinforce your brand. This also includes teaching your employees the power of stories and how to share them. That's what we'll discuss next.

Check and reflect

- Do you know exactly how you would want your brand described?

- Do you have a stated company purpose and values?

- Do all your employees understand what the desired brand is?

- Are they aware of how their daily actions can organically strengthen or weaken the organisational brand?

TEACH
HOW TO EDUCATE
STORYTELLERS

A woman at one of my training sessions told me about a time that she had shared a story in a business situation. She said it was a bit personal and certainly showed vulnerability, but she told me it didn't work. In fact, she received feedback that the story was inappropriate. Some of her team even laughed at her, which sounds horrendous ... and guess what? She never tried storytelling again. When I hear stories like this it really saddens me.

Maya Angelou said, 'There is no greater agony than bearing an untold story inside you', and that is true. But having the courage to share a story and not doing it effectively because you didn't know how, and being scared to the point you never try it again ... now that *is* agony.

> *The choice for leaders in business and organisations is not whether to be involved in storytelling, they can hardly do otherwise, but rather whether to use storytelling unwittingly and clumsily or intelligently and skilfully.*

This quote is from Stephen Denning's book *The Leader's Guide to Storytelling*, which is a book that changed my life. It was one of the catalysts for me leaving my corporate life and embarking on a mission to teach businesspeople how to use stories intelligently and skilfully, and not, as Steve puts it, clumsily and unwittingly.

Denning's book, and this quote specifically, reinforced to me that storytelling is a critical business capability, but also a skill that can be taught.

Storytelling is a skill. Like any other skill, some people may be naturally better at it than others, just like some people are naturally better at tennis, drawing or cooking than others. However, with the right teaching, guidance and practice we can all get better at anything ... including storytelling.

I think it's irresponsible for organisations to ask their people to share stories but not educate them on how to do it; it's setting them up for failure.

If you want to learn how to play the piano, it would probably be a good idea to get some lessons. If you want your team members to start using a new accounting system, you should probably invest in training them. If your team were pretty good at presenting but they needed to be better, you would probably also invest in training ... you get the point.

IF YOU WANT YOUR TEAM TO TELL MAGNETIC STORIES ABOUT YOUR BRAND THEN YOU HAVE TO TEACH THEM HOW TO DO THAT.

Imagine ... and realise

Imagine if, at the start of each team meeting, you opened with someone sharing a story of a core value. Perhaps the value is 'delighting our customers', and someone shares the story of John in the New York store who saw a customer struggle with their luggage in the rain, so rushed over with his own umbrella to help her and her luggage into a taxi.

Then the team leader shares that story at their meeting with their peers, which escalates the story up to the next level. Depending on the size of the company, it could be cascaded up a few more levels. On hearing that story, perhaps the CEO or a senior executive contacts John to let him know how proud she was to hear about what he did for that customer on that rainy day. How his actions truly demonstrate the value of delighting customers.

How do you think John feels on receiving that call? And what do you think he does next?

I think he would feel pretty good. I think he would feel engaged. I think he would feel appreciated and that his actions had been acknowledged. I also think he might tell his colleagues about getting a call from the CEO. I think he would also go home and tell his family. And you know what else he will do? The very next day he will be actively looking for opportunities to delight customers once again … as will the colleagues that he shared the story with.

THIS TYPE OF COMMITMENT FROM THE ORGANISATION ENCOURAGES DESIRED BEHAVIOUR AND STORY SHARING, WHICH ENCOURAGES MORE DESIRED BEHAVIOURS, GENERATES MORE STORIES, AND SO ON.

This would lead to some pretty engaged employees and connected customers, don't you think?

But this won't happen by just imagining it. You've got to teach everyone the power of storytelling and how to share stories effectively to make this a reality.

So let's look at how to do that.

Who do you teach?

One of the first questions organisations grapple with when they contemplate introducing storytelling is who needs the training? Is it just the CEO and executive leadership team? Is it all leaders? Is it marketing and corporate affairs? Maybe it's the sales and relationship management team? What about the frontline, customer-facing people? Is it all employees?

The answer depends on what you want to achieve. Some organisations simply want to increase their leaders' ability to communicate and influence better, so maybe it's just the leaders. Some want to use stories when pitching for work as a way to stand out from their competitors; in that case, it's only the sales and relationship management people.

HOWEVER, IF YOU WANT TO INTRODUCE BRAND STORYTELLING IN A REAL EFFORT TO CONNECT WITH CUSTOMERS AND ENGAGE EMPLOYEES, THEN ALL EMPLOYEES NEED SOME LEVEL OF EDUCATION AROUND STORIES.

... And how?

Employees who have more influence and opportunity to share stories will need more intense training than those who don't.

Regardless, there are four key guidelines to follow to teach the right people in your organisation the valuable skill of storytelling. These guidelines are all based on my 15 years' experience of seeing what works and what doesn't:

1. Ensure senior executives are involved in the training.

2. Train all leaders.

3. Train key support staff.

4. Ensure training involves the practice of sharing stories.

Ensure senior executives are involved in the training

To ensure success with storytelling, ideally the skills training should start with the senior leaders and cascade down to lower levels. While the order isn't crucial, it is very important for the senior leaders to be skilled up.

Training the senior executives on how to share stories more effectively has multiple benefits.

First, they actually get better at communicating their messages in a more engaging way — in a way people can actually understand and remember.

Second, through the process of sharing their own stories, they are seen to be more 'human' and 'approachable'.

Third, they role-model storytelling. When other people see their most senior leaders sharing stories, this gives them the encouragement and permission to do the same. We need to accept the current situation: for the vast majority of our careers in business we have been told to 'show the facts' and that 'business isn't personal'. Because of this, it may take some encouragement for some of the more reluctant leaders to show a more personal side.

Train all leaders

While you should train the senior executives for all the reasons just discussed, you shouldn't train *only* the senior executives. It's normally the next few layers down of leaders that have the greatest day-to-day influence in engaging employees.

But team leaders can be a difficult bunch to get in a training room. Just the sheer demands on their time make it difficult to get them for a few hours. However, one of the aspects I touch on when training leaders in storytelling is the power in being able to step into vulnerability. Sometimes ego prevents them from wanting to do something in front of their peers that they are not very good at. This inability to be vulnerable is often the reason that they won't even get to the training room. Of course, there will be other excuses cited, such as 'I don't need it', 'I'm already good at it' and 'I don't need stories because I work in finance, technology, medicine, etc.'

Leaders tend to fall into four categories when learning storytelling:

1. **Sceptical.** These are the people who think they don't need it at all because they 'deal with data and numbers'. (I see this a lot in finance and technology.)

2. **Reluctant.** These people believe they are already good at it. That they have been 'doing it all their life', so they don't see the need to undertake any form of training.

3. **Curious.** They are not totally sure how they would use storytelling but they're willing to find out. They know the benefits of storytelling and come to the training with an open mind.

4. **Eager.** They are the ones who are keen to get better at storytelling. They know it will help them improve the way they communicate and influence, and they really want to keep developing that capability.

Over the last 15 years the percentage in each group has changed. Fifteen years ago, there were more people who were sceptical and reluctant but, as storytelling has become more accepted as a business skill, the vast majority are now in the curious and eager camp — which is good news you should capitalise on!

Train key support staff

Besides training the leaders, make sure you also include key support people from human resources, corporate affairs and marketing, as well as other key influencers across the organisation. This allows them to support and encourage the use of storytelling throughout the organisation. Many companies I work with provide additional training for these support people so they can take on the informal role as internal storytelling advocates.

They can also better share stories for some of the more traditional communication channels we discuss later, such as social media and newsletters.

A mistake I see some organisations make is *only* educating the support staff. When this happens, it sends a very clear signal that the responsibility of communicating and sharing brand stories is theirs alone, when it is actually everyone's responsibility.

Another mistake is not training anyone. An example of this was a few years back when I was asked to train the top 40 leaders of an organisation in storytelling, to help them communicate the company's strategy. The strategy had been communicated about six months prior but the CEO was concerned that his most senior leaders could not explain it properly.[1] Working with the senior leaders (including the CEO) to help them gain clarity on the messages and then how to communicate them in an effective and engaging way through their own stories is a brilliant way to approach this. Except the person who asked me to do this work was overruled by the head of marketing. What they decided to do was create one story that all the senior leaders would share. This is not such a brilliant idea. In fact, it's a terrible idea! It's akin to rote learning ... which is perfectly fine if you're learning your times table, but not if you are trying to communicate a complex strategy to all employees.

---

[1] Which makes me think that he did not explain it properly to his senior leaders ... just saying.

The company then asked me to quote on giving one-on-one mentoring to each of the senior leaders so they could better recite this story. I refused to provide a quote, knowing this had failure written all over it.

Ensure training involves the practice of sharing stories

During my training, I spend a lot of time helping participants understand the practicalities behind storytelling: why it works. What actually makes a story a story ... because, as we have discussed, calling something a story does not make it a story. I teach them a framework on how to get clear on their message, where to find stories and then how to construct them ... how to start them, what to put in the middle and how to end it to ensure it gets the message across without being directive. Then the most critical part is for them to share their story. This verbal sharing of stories with each other is a critical aspect of my training programs, for several reasons.

First, it actually provides a safe environment for them to practice. Sharing stories involves vulnerability, and people are often surprised by how nervous they get before sharing their stories. Sometimes sharing stories brings up unexpected emotions, and this needs to happen in a safe environment.

Second, everyone gets to experience the power of the stories. I always ask after this story-sharing session what people liked about it, and inevitably I receive a variety of the following responses:

- **'I really enjoyed hearing other people's stories.'** This is an insight for a lot of people who think their stories aren't interesting or important enough.

- **'I was surprised by the impact some of the stories had on me. At one point I got a bit emotional.'** Even the most sceptical people are not immune to the power of stories (because they are human), and when they experience the impact they start to feel for themselves what stories can do.

- **'I feel a closer connection with the people who shared their stories with me.'** I would never advertise my storytelling training as a team building or bonding activity, but one of the amazing benefits of this process is that is exactly what happens. Teams walk out of the session with a closer relationship. They experience firsthand what all the research we discussed earlier tells us. That we create a stronger connection with the story and the storyteller. That the stories can strengthen relationships and build trust ... creating an initial magnetic attraction that is hard to disconnect from.

ONCE THE TRAINING HAS HAPPENED IT'S IMPORTANT TO KEEP THE MOMENTUM GOING BY CREATING ADDITIONAL OPPORTUNITIES FOR THE LEADERS TO PRACTISE SHARING STORIES.

This not only helps them improve their storytelling capability but also continues the sharing process. One way to do this is to implement a story share moment at the start of team meetings, where one or two people share a story. Companies that have a strong emphasis on safety have been doing this for decades. Maybe pick a value of the month and ask for stories on that.

The initial training and a continuing process to maintain momentum starts the collect and communicate process that we discuss next.

When organisations take educating their employees in storytelling seriously and implement processes to keep the momentum going, then, over time, storytelling becomes second nature. When this happens people will start to pay attention to the stories they are hearing. They will start to become better at digging deeper to find the good stories and they will help share these stories so they reach as many people as possible.

Check and reflect

- Do your employees understand the power of brand storytelling?

- Have your leaders been given an opportunity to personally connect with the company's values?

- Have leaders been trained to communicate purpose, values and strategy through personal stories?

- Have all relevant support professionals also been trained in storytelling to encourage the use of stories and help collect and communicate them?

COLLECT
HOW TO FIND STORIES

When people ask me how I find stories to share, I often use the analogy that I'm like those people who walk along the beach with a metal detector. But instead of looking for and finding metal, I look for and find stories.

STORIES ARE ALWAYS THERE, BUT THEY'RE HIDDEN UNDER THE SURFACE AND YOU NEED TO KNOW WHEN AND WHERE TO DIG A BIT DEEPER.

Teaching your leaders and other key people in your organisation about your brand, its messages, and storytelling on the whole, will also start the collecting process, but there is a process you can follow to uncover more.

It very rarely is as easy as asking someone to 'tell me a story'. That's a common mistake. Most people think that what they did or what they achieved is not big enough to be considered a story that others would want to hear. You need to draw it out of them and draw out the relevant details.

If your organisation has been around for a while, let's say more than 50 years, and you want to uncover the stories from your past (which you should!), then you may have to allocate someone to go through historic records to uncover specific events and backstories. These are the heritage stories discussed in part I. Two companies we look at in the case stories, The Fullerton Hotels and Resorts and Columbia Restaurant, do just that, with Columbia Restaurants actually hiring a journalist to research for them.

If you are a smaller company or a younger start-up, it's unlikely you'd need to employ someone, but you absolutely will need a process to find and draw out both past and present stories.

There are several ways to start finding and collecting stories to consider. So let's look at those now so you can see which ones are relevant to you.

Finding current stories

To find stories from the present you need to undertake a process to find examples of when employees have:

- lived by the company's values

- demonstrated the desired behaviours

- made decisions in line with your brand.

This could be the CEO making an organisation-wide decision, or a casual worker going above and beyond to deliver something.

The process I follow is called 'story-finding sessions'. I have used this process over the last 15 years to uncover some very powerful magnetic stories.

You ideally want an experienced facilitator to run these sessions: one who will be able to create a safe environment where people are willing to share stories and will also know when to dig a bit deeper with the right questions.

You should include a diverse group of people in your company who would be willing to contribute in these sessions. Ensure when you look at diversity it goes beyond gender, race and age. You should also look for diversity in terms of:

- **Tenure.** You want people who are relatively new to the company so they can share very recent experiences through to employees who have been around for years. That way you could uncover some of those powerful heritage stories.

- **Hierarchy.** Try to get a good mix of senior leaders through to more junior people. Depending on the culture and how safe it is for more junior people to speak freely in front of senior management, you may wish to run several sessions with more junior employees in one group and more senior in another. Even with the most open and transparent senior leaders, there still may be reluctance.

- **Department.** You should aim to get people from various departments in the company, including customer-facing roles, support roles and back-end roles.

- **Location.** Depending on how many geographical locations you have, you may want to run these sessions in each location.

Aim for a practical number of people in each session, about ten to 15, to allow everyone a chance to participate. A good length of time for the session is two hours.

Always provide catering afterwards such as morning tea, lunch, afternoon tea or drinks. (There is a reason for this that I will explain a bit later.)

Questions to ask

Once you've got a session organised, you're going to craft a set of questions that will elicit stories from the people attending. Some questions will be more directed at what you have defined your brand to be. For example, if you have defined integrity as part of your brand you may say, 'Describe a time when you or someone in your team spoke out against something that didn't seem right.' Or, 'Describe a time when you or a colleague were asked to do something but refused to do it on principle.' If you are looking for brand stories around safety, you may want to say, 'Describe a time when someone spoke up about a concern that averted a problem.'

Other prompts may be more generic, such as, 'Tell me about a time you were proud to work here.' These questions can trigger revealing stories.

Some prompts that I have used to great effect include:

- When have you seen a colleague help a customer in a way that has made a difference?

- Describe a time when you or a colleague went out of their way to help a customer.

- Describe a time when you or someone you know at work did the right thing for another employee.

- Tell us about a team member of yours that is doing something good in the community that they should be acknowledged for.

- Share an example of when you saw a small change make a difference in a client's or colleague's life.

- Describe a positive experience a customer has told you they have had with us.

- Describe a positive experience a supplier has said they have had with us.

- Share a time when you felt happy and proud to work here.

- Give us an example of something you have seen or heard recently at work that inspired you.

- Share a time when you went home excited about something that had happened at work.

You will notice that the word 'story' does not appear in any of these prompts.

What I have found is when you ask people to tell a story, for example 'Can you tell us a story about customer service?' people seem to draw a blank. Using the word 'story' makes them think that it has to be this big grand event, and they then dismiss all the examples they are thinking of.

I GUARANTEE THAT BY ASKING THESE QUESTIONS, PEOPLE WILL, BY DEFAULT, TELL YOU A STORY.

You may choose to send the questions to the invited participants a day or two beforehand. This provides them with just the right amount of thinking time. When you send the questions, state clearly that they do not have to come prepared with an answer to each question; they are simply thought-provokers. Alternatively, just hand the questions out at the start of the session.

Facilitating story-finding sessions

On the day of the session, start by explaining:

- the concept of storytelling

- why you are choosing to collect stories to communicate the company's brand

- what you hope to use some of the stories for.

IT'S A GOOD IDEA TO RECORD THE STORIES, SO ADVISE PARTICIPANTS THAT YOU WILL BE AUDIO RECORDING THE STORIES TO HELP WITH TRANSCRIBING LATER.

Provide a basic framework on how to tell a story. This is not the full education workshop, just some basics of asking them to keep the stories relatively short (a few minutes), as you will ask follow-up questions if need be. Also ask them to start with when this happened and where.

Share an example of your own story, role-modelling the length and structure. Then ask people to share a story of theirs and start recording.

To help track stories, write down the storyteller's name and briefly what the story was about. This will help with identifying the stories and person who shared it later.

Ask follow-up questions if appropriate. A good question is 'How did that make you feel?' Sometimes the natural reaction in a business setting is to provide more detail of what they *did*; if this is the case, keep asking, 'How did that make you feel?'

This process needs to be facilitated well to ensure everyone gets a chance to contribute. Also, if stories start going longer and longer (this naturally happens) then remind people to keep it to a few minutes.

Once everyone has shared a story, then just keep going. This is when it will become more organic and a story will spark another story. People will just keep jumping in with, 'Yes I had a similar experience ... '

With about five or ten minutes remaining in the session, ask them which stories really resonated with them the most. Which stories will they likely retell? Make a note of this because this is an indication of the 'magnetic-ness' of some of the stories.

In a two-hour session you may hear 30 to 50 stories, but there may only be five or ten you will want to collect and share more widely.

Invite them to stay for morning tea or lunch. Every time I have done this, over this additional 30 minutes or so is where I hear some real gems. I'm not sure what it is, but I suspect that people let their guard down and share more willingly once the pressure of the formal session is lifted.

It could also be that after 90 minutes or so they have built up trust and a relationship with people in the room, which happens when you use stories. Whatever the science behind it, I know it works, hence why I always include that bit of social gathering afterwards so people are not rushing off to their next meeting.

Analysing after the session

After the session, you'll decide which stories warrant being documented. You have the original recording, but for the stories that have been selected you may want to transcribe them into a written format. You can then send it back to the person who told the story, seeking any clarification and sign-off for accuracy.

You now have this in written format. Depending on what you are planning to do with the stories, you may want to go back to the storytellers at a later date and record them on video or audio.

You'll also want to analyse the types of stories you heard. Were they predominantly positive stories about safety? If so, this would indicate that there is a strong safety culture. Were there some questions that no-one could really provide an example of? If this is the case it may mean that this value is not necessary a reality. It might just mean that you need to invest more effort in ensuring that value is raised in importance.

I once ran this session for a client who had a value of integrity, yet not one example emerged about this — even though I asked some specific questions about it!

On the other hand, a couple of years ago my accounting firm, which had been expanding over the years, wanted to do some work on defining their purpose and values. Knowing what I did, they asked me to help. So I facilitated a story-finding session with the team following the process I've just walked you through.

As I heard the stories coming from the prepared questions, I took note of the stories that seemed to have the biggest impact on the team. I started to see patterns emerge with the stories. Towards the end we took a break and I loosely categorised the stories based on these themes that had been emerging.

After the break I told them about the grouping of stories and wanted to know if they believed the following represented their values:

- Everyone has a voice.

- Everyone gets stuck in.

- We deliver on promises.

- We take on the impossible.

- Everyone brings their genius.

There was a resounding response of 'we think that perfectly sums us up'.

They only made slight changes to the wording before they produced some banners to place around the office. (What I also like is that they resisted the urge to shorten these into one word, which many companies do but it tends to strip them of all meaning.)

BASED ON THE ANALYSIS YOU WILL HAVE A GOOD INDICATION OF WHICH VALUES ARE ALREADY EMBEDDED AND PART OF YOUR BRAND. YOU WILL ALSO KNOW WHICH VALUES NEED A BIT OF WORK.

An additional benefit of these sessions is the people in the room will walk out feeling so proud. Their engagement will go through the roof.

I recall one time I facilitated one of these sessions with employees from the call centre of a bank. I brought along my executive manager, Elise, who was so impressed with the stories she said to me, 'I want to work for them in the call centre!' She was joking (I think), but then she said seriously, 'I never knew the bank did these things — why don't they share these good things they do?' A very valid question.

Regardless of the process you follow to find these stories, you should find them. Think of your organisational stories like a rock band's Greatest Hits album. The longer the organisation goes on, the more songs they produce. And assuming they are good songs, they will keep adding volumes II and III, and so on, to their Greatest Hits collections.

These Greatest Hits stories can be shared internally to engage employees and externally to connect with customers — and in a whole heap of ways. Which perfectly leads into the next section: how to communicate the stories.

Check and reflect

- Do you have a process of finding culture stories of employees living the brand?

- Have you investigated any stories from the past that would be significant enough to share today?

- How are you collecting these stories to ensure they are not lost in the future?

- Do you have a diversity of stories that reflect all elements of your brand or are there gaps?

COMMUNICATE
WHERE TO SHARE STORIES

Once you have taken the time to find your stories, you then need to share them — otherwise, what's the point? There's a wide variety of ways to share stories: the only limitation is your imagination.

For example, a footwear company based in Melbourne has the backstory of the name of their company written on a pair of shoes.[1]

> *The Django and Juliette footwear brand is the brainchild of Kerrie Munro. With the arrival of her twin nephew and niece in 2001, who were uniquely named Django and Juliette respectively, a distinctive footwear brand was born in Melbourne, Australia at the same time.*

Some companies get very creative with sharing their stories in physical places, such as The Fullerton Hotel Singapore, which has a dedicated heritage gallery space in the lobby. Or on the menu, like the Columbia Restaurant in Florida in the United States. (More on both of these in the case stories.)

You need to communicate stories both internally and externally. A story on your website or LinkedIn has the potential to connect and engage both your customers and your employees … and let's not forget potential customers and employees.

Some stories may only ever be shared via internal channels, such as your induction process or Yammer or Workspace. However, the employees may

---

[1] And yes, I bought a pair.

share the stories externally, even if it's just with their family and friends. This is the Glass Box theory mentioned in the introduction.

In this chapter, I want to focus on some of the best (but often underused) ways to communicate stories, both internally and externally. Hopefully it might give you some ideas.

AS THE SUBTITLE OF THIS BOOK IMPLIES, SHARING MAGNETIC STORIES ABOUT YOUR BRAND IS ALL ABOUT CONNECTING WITH CUSTOMERS AND ENGAGING EMPLOYEES.

So let's look at some ways and places you can do just that.

Induction

The whole purpose of induction programs is to integrate new employees into the company in the most effective and efficient way. Basically, give them everything they need to be doing their job, as soon as possible. But it is also one of the most effective places to use stories to engage employees and get them understanding the culture of the organisation from day one.

While induction training should cover the processes and systems and include key information on health and safety, it should also cover the values and behaviours expected of the new employee. This applies whether it's a formal induction training program or an informal 'showing people the ropes' one.

THE STORIES YOUR NEW EMPLOYEES HEAR DURING THEIR INDUCTION CAN HAVE THE POWER TO ENGAGE THEM RIGHT FROM THE START.

National Australia Bank (NAB) have been a long-term client of mine. I worked for them for 17 years, starting as a trainee computer operator back in 1988. When I left, they were my first client (thanks, Kate and Phil) back in 2005 — and I still work with various leaders across the bank to this very day. In 2018, the NAB team revamped their induction program to focus on establishing a shared understanding of the culture of NAB. It was important to Melissa Grasso, then the Head of Culture Development, and the delivery team (including Jennifer Gosden) that this understanding was more than intellectual, and actually resonated with people on an emotional level.

Up until COVID-19 took hold, all new Australia-based employees, regardless of position or location, were invited to attend a one-day induction program called Welcome to NAB. It wasn't on their first day at the company, but relatively soon after they had started. Welcome to NAB was all about the purpose and values of the company. It was hosted by an internal facilitator, with one or two senior leaders running the day, and additional facilitators running immersion sessions on each value.

This is a program that appreciates the power of stories: throughout the day participants regularly engaged with thought-provoking or emotionally impactful stories from NAB's customers, colleagues and senior leaders. Given that senior leaders have a particularly critical role in bringing NAB's strategy and purpose to life, storytelling training was offered to all of the leaders who were involved in hosting the Welcome to NAB program. This gave them the opportunity to improve their overall communication capability in ways that could be applied in all aspects of their role.

After attending storytelling training, leaders were given guidance by the delivery team on how the induction day would run, the messages they needed to deliver and the types of stories they needed to prepare, followed by a coaching session a few weeks prior to the day to refine their stories. The day before was a rehearsal where they received feedback and a run-through to integrate the feedback. The rehearsal was filmed so leaders could further review their delivery. Leaders regularly mentioned that, while it was hard to view their recordings, it was helpful for realising how they came across. Even the leaders most experienced at public speaking benefited from the attention to practice. This level of support for leaders was implemented after Jennifer reviewed the delivery of the first few programs, and saw the potential to create greater impact with additional preparation on leaders' stories.

While leaders focused on work-related stories to bring the strategy to life, they were encouraged to start the day with a purpose-related story and relevant accompanying photo from their personal life. The intent was to connect first as people, as personal stories remove potential barriers that seniority can often create. Leaders sharing pictures with their family on holiday, playing their favourite sport or coaching basketball made them instantly more relatable. This approach was well received by participants and helped to set a warm and open tone for the day.

The decision to revamp the induction program around stories was intentional. Melissa believed it provided quite a few benefits for the company, the leaders involved and the participants in the induction program. For the leaders, the benefit was they were better able to articulate the company's purpose and values, not only to the people on the induction program but also to their teams.

The stories enabled new employees to better understand the NAB's purpose, strategy and values, and genuinely connect to them. As well, it meant they connected better with the leaders who shared the stories. The barrier that a title can sometimes erect was broken down through the stories.

Michelle Obama put this best when she said,

> I tell people we focus too much on stats and not story. If we can open up a little bit more to each other and share our stories — our real stories — that's what breaks down barriers.

The Key Speech

The stories shared at induction also do not have to be from current leaders. Take for example the design and architect firm Arup.

As part of their induction to Arup all employees are required to read a speech that was given by their founder, Ove Arup, in 1970. Called the 'Key Speech' it is also displayed on their website as well as used in the induction process.

SoftwareONE, a global technology solutions company headquartered in Switzerland, also show a video at induction and other internal programs of their founder Patrick Winter, who passed away in 2018. In this video Patrick talks about the company's purpose and values.

Consider what stories you could share with new employees that will get them engaged in the purpose and values of the company.

You don't want induction programs to be only about showing new employees where the kitchen and stationery cupboard is. You also don't want to just be telling new employees what the values are; you need to communicate them with stories to give them meaning.

Remember, an induction program is not just for large organisations. Regardless of your organisation's size, it's worth thinking of the stories that you share with new employees from day one. The CEO of Ferguson Plarre Bakehouses, Steve Plarre, allocates 30 minutes to every new employee to share the creation stories from his fifth-generation family business (more about that in the case stories).

I didn't want to leave the reflection process to the end of this chapter, so after each channel I'm going to ask you three questions.

Three questions to consider

1. What creation story do you have that every employee should know about?

2. What culture stories of employees living the values could show new employees the behaviours that are expected?

3. What community, challenge or customer stories do you have that will help employees bond with your brand?

Published writing — newsletters, emails and annual reports

Don't make the mistake of sharing stories once in only one format; find places to share them in newsletters, emails and other printed publications. Stories in the written format can be an effective way to reach your customers and employees.

MANY COMPANIES ARE STARTING TO REALISE THE IMPORTANCE OF INCLUDING STORIES IN THEIR ANNUAL REPORT, AS WELL AS ALL THE USUAL FINANCIAL REPORTS AND REGULATORY REQUIREMENTS.

Remember SisterWorks, an organisation I introduced you to earlier? They take the opportunity in their annual report and website to share the stories of many of the members they support.

One such story in their annual report included Manaka from Japan:

> *Manaka was only 9 years old when she came to Australia with her mother and sisters. Now qualified with a BA in Food Science and a passion for food, Manaka took the opportunity to volunteer at SisterWorks as Food Production Assistant. She enjoyed her time in the SisterWorks production kitchen but wanted more challenges so she signed up as Food-tasting Coordinator, assisting the Sales Manager to organise tastings at Ritchies Supermarkets.*
>
> *SisterWorks then offered Manaka a paid position of Cooking Training in their Cooking Lab, which led to Manaka taking over as Food Production Lead.*
>
> *Manaka is a woman with many skills and loves challenges, as she's now also learning about managing individuals as well as teams. These skills will assist her to achieve her ultimate dream job in Food Product Development.*

Three questions to consider

1. How could you incorporate stories into your annual report or other written materials to make them more interesting?

2. Which customer could you showcase in your report by sharing their story?

3. What challenge did you face in the last 12 months that you could include?

Short movies

Creating a movie for your company might seem a bit left-of-field and a time-consuming and costly project, but it's exactly what oil and gas company Apache Corporation did in 2019.

In November 2017, Apache introduced a new vision. They didn't want the vision to be purely aspirational, as most are — they wanted it to be inspirational for their employees.

Anne Hedrich was part of the communication campaign to share this new vision with employees and there was a deliberate approach to use storytelling to do that.

Anne interviewed employees across each of Apache's main locations to bring the company's vision and culture to life in their own words. The end result was a 30-minute documentary-style short movie, titled *The Path to Premier,* that they debuted internally for their employees.

Initially, they had planned to hire out movie theatres to show the movie, but in the end they turned each main office location into a global movie experience complete with popcorn and hot dogs. They also added Hollywood Walk of Fame–style stars on the floor with the names of the featured employees.

They even created a short 'coming soon' trailer, as well as movie posters of some of the employees featured … which seriously made them look like movie stars.

Anne said the whole experience generated a lot of excitement and unity amongst the employees, emphasising that every role was important to the success of the company.

The Columbia Restaurant Group (featured in the case stories) also commissioned a film to be made about a restaurant they purchased: Goody Goody, a drive-in restaurant that opened in 1925 in Tampa, Florida. The president of the Columbia Restaurant Group, Richard Gonzmart, and his family were huge fans of Goody Goody for decades. So they purchased the rights to Goody Goody, including the name, recipes, signs, furniture, photos and memorabilia after the previous owner closed it in 2005 and the building was pulled down. The 45-minute feature film follows how Goody

Goody started, what it meant to local residents and how devasted they were when it closed in 2005, through to the Columbia Restaurant Group rebuilding it and reopening it in 2016.[2]

Three questions to consider

1. Is there anything a bit unusual in your company that would warrant making a short movie about?

2. What would be the purpose of it?

3. Once produced, on what other channels could you share it, such as your induction program, website or social media?

Website

I met a woman a couple of years ago who ran a number of childcare centres. She used to be a dentist, so I was intrigued how she made that career change. She told me that she took a long time to fall pregnant with her son Joe. When she was thinking about going back to work she started looking at a few childcare centres and was unhappy with what she saw. So she bought one and turned it into a childcare centre that Joe would be happy in. Everyone who works for her knows this story, to the point that when decisions are made about the centres they ask themselves: 'Would this make Joe happy?' Even though Joe is now at school and no longer in childcare, the message of the story is not lost.

THINK ABOUT IT FOR A MINUTE: HOW DOES THIS STORY MAKE YOU FEEL? WHAT DOES IT TELL YOU ABOUT THE COMPANY'S BRAND AND WHAT THEY VALUE?

Would hearing this story have an impact on your final decision of what childcare centre to choose? I know if I were looking for a childcare centre and read that story I would be saying 'sign me up'.

---

[2] You can view it on Columbia Restaurant's YouTube channel.

Many businesses miss a great opportunity by not putting their creation story on their website, instead putting up a jargon-laden paragraph that explains nothing. Your website is often one of the first interactions people will have with your brand. Why not share a selection of stories on your website from the five types we speak about in part II to create that instant connection? Most of the stories in this book are featured on their company's website.

The stories can be either written or on video. Who Gives A Crap has a great video on their website on how they started — look it up.

I don't have a strong opinion on what is better; personally, I have done both with slightly different content. The real key is to make sure the stories on your website are not just a timeline of the company.

Three questions to consider

1. What stories could you include on your website — e.g. a creation story in the 'About Us' section?

2. What culture or community stories demonstrating your company's values could you use on your website?

3. What stories do you have about your customers that talk about what you do and how you do it that could be featured on your website? Perhaps it could be an interview with them?

Social media

The global accounting firm EY introduced 'Flextober' a few years ago: during the month of October employees are encouraged to share on social media what working flexibly has enabled them to do. This company wants to be known for their flexible working conditions, so they encourage employees to take selfies and post about it on their personal social media page, such as LinkedIn and Facebook. You will often see other employees then sharing, liking and commenting on these posts.

I hear many stories about the good things companies are doing because their employees have shared them on their personal social media sites.

Give permission and encourage your own employees to share stories that communicate the company brand. Both your internal and external social media channels can be a great way to do this.

As social media platforms evolve it's a good idea to keep abreast of what platforms allow you to more effectively share your stories. Instagram is increasingly being used by businesses to share brand stories. And in 2020 TikTok launched TikTok For Business to allow brands to communicate their stories in a more creative and engaging way.

YOU DON'T WANT YOUR SOCIAL MEDIA TO FEEL FORCED, LIKE ADVERTISING, BUT YOU DON'T WANT YOUR POLICY TO BE SO RISK-AVERSE AND COMPLICATED THAT EMPLOYEES DON'T KNOW WHAT THEY CAN AND CANNOT SHARE.

Three questions to consider

1. Do you encourage your employees to actively share stories on their personal LinkedIn or other social media sites?

2. Are there social media platforms that you could use more effectively to share your brand stories?

3. Are there customer stories that you could share via social media to amplify their voice?

Presentations, interviews and speeches

In 2016 Sheryl Sandberg, Chief Operating Officer at Facebook and author of the best-selling book *Lean In*, delivered the commencement speech at California's Berkeley University.

Her 25-minute speech included no fewer than ten stories and numerous examples to support her messages. Within the first few minutes of her speech, she shared a story about her grandmother who attended Berkeley in the 1970s, becoming the first college graduate in her family. She also silenced the crowd with 'One year and 13 days ago, I lost my husband Dave.' The story of her husband's death demonstrated courage, vulnerability and learning through times of adversity. While this story was only a couple of minutes in length, she referred back to it several times throughout her speech to bring to life the messages she wanted to communicate.

I often have business leaders ask me, 'How many stories is enough?' After seeing Sandberg's speech I think the answer is 'there are never too many', especially if they are relevant, engaging and well told. Sadly, in the business world we are far away from too many stories. On the spectrum of too many bullet points versus too many stories, unfortunately we are still at the bullet point end of the spectrum. Which is not very engaging.

Presentations don't always have to be the same format. Sometimes when I work with clients to help them with their presentation, I suggest, 'Why don't you do it in interview style as opposed to presenting?' The reason I do this is because the interviewer asking the right questions will result in stories being shared. The interviewer can ask additional questions of the subject that will draw out more stories than perhaps would have been shared in a traditional presentation.

I remember I learnt this lesson early on in my storytelling career when I worked with Rob Jager, who was the Chairman of Shell Companies based in New Zealand. Rob was also going to be speaking to the leaders on leadership, values and behaviours, and I was asked to help him with his presentation: help him be clear on his messages and the stories he would share.

I actually can't recall who suggested an interview over a presentation, but we decided that I would interview him on stage. We still knew what messages we wanted to communicate and we had planned most of the questions while still leaving room for spontaneity. And this is exactly what happened. On stage Rob was more relaxed, and when needed I could ask follow-up questions to dig deeper into his stories.

So even though this was prepared, it came across as more genuine and it was definitely more engaging.

Three questions to consider

1. What is the main theme of your presentation, and which personal story could you start with that will connect with the audience straight away?

2. Which culture stories can you weave in to communicate your messages but also reinforce your brand?

3. Does your presentation need to be a presentation or would an interview format allow more stories to be shared, which would potentially be more engaging?

Customer interactions

Remember Kim Seagram from the gin distillery in Tasmania? I contacted her to talk to her about stories. She said that while she was trained as a biologist she understands that when it comes to marketing, 'stories are more effective than advertising'. She believes that through stories you 'build a community' and that 'people form an attraction to you through the stories, not the products and services you are selling'. She added that 'stories make people want to be a part of what you are doing'.

Kim started to realise this when she opened Stillwater restaurant in the Tamar Valley in 2000. With an ambition to put Tasmania on the map as a world-class dining destination, she was passionate about sourcing local supplies. She said it wasn't about telling her story but sharing the stories of Tasmania and the produce on their plate. Kim said, 'I could share stories all evening with diners about the butter that was on their plate, the venison or wallaby they were eating, the local wine and beer ... I could even share stories about the table they were sitting at that was made from local timber.'

Kim believes that it is these stories that elevate a meal to a dining experience, and through the stories there is a greater connection to and appreciation of her customers.

Relationship-based customer interactions, such as those that happen in the hospitality industry, provide more opportunities to share stories. Professional service firms or consultants that work with clients over a long period will also find more opportunities to share stories than in transactional customer interactions. (I don't need to hear a story every time I buy a carton of milk or fill up my car with petrol!)

Three questions to consider

1. What stories can your frontline employees share with customers to connect with them better?

2. Which stories would enhance your customer's experience?

3. What stories could be shared that would enhance your brand?

Sales pitches

Stories can also help you connect with potential customers, so sales pitches and meetings are another obvious place to share stories. As Seth Godin says, 'Marketing is no longer about the stuff that you make but about the stories you tell.'

Many of my clients work with me to help them use stories more effectively in their sales pitches. When they go in to pitch for work, they understand that their competitors are potentially pitching a 95 per cent similar approach — and that they can potentially sway a buyer when they create a human connection.

You may have been in the position before of speaking to several suppliers before making a decision. You probably found, before you even worked through which one it logically made sense to hire, that you had sort of already made the decision on an emotional basis because you liked one more than the others. I can almost guarantee you they shared stories with you that fast-tracked the connection and the relationship and created that 'I like you' moment.

WE LIKE WORKING WITH PEOPLE WE LIKE AND CONNECT WITH — WHICH IS HOW STORIES CAN HELP.

Three questions to consider

1. What stories could you share in a pitch that demonstrate values that you know your potential client also shares?

2. Which stories do you have that engage on a human level (as opposed to case studies that just educate)?

3. What stories could you share in those informal times before and after the meeting that could create that 'I like you' moment?

I hope this chapter has provided you with some food for thought in all the different ways you can communicate your brand stories. This hasn't covered every single possible way or place you could communicate a story, so I will leave you with three final questions to consider.

Check and reflect

- Which of these channels do you use well, but could do more of?

- Which of these had you not thought of, but could use?

- Where else could you share your stories?[3]

---

[3] If you have shared brand stories in another unique way I would love you to tell me about it. Ways to reach me can be found at the end of the book!

CREATE
HOW TO GENERATE STORIES

The previous chapter explores some of the various ways you can communicate your stories, but I deliberately left one out.

This is not your normal 'channel' of communication, yet it is the one that is often the most influential. It can potentially reach more people then you ever thought you could.

It doesn't cost any money to share your stories in it. And it can as easily build up your brand or completely destroy it.

It's called the grapevine.

Every single person you interact with is part of the grapevine. Colleagues, clients, potential clients, employees, potential employees, suppliers, partners, competitors ... everyone.

The term 'grapevine' originates from the American Civil War when telegraph lines where strung from tree to tree, like vines. It was popularised by Marvin Gaye when in 1968 he released the song 'I heard it through the grapevine', which reached number one in the United States and the UK.

Grapevine communication is informal conversations between people.

IT DOES NOT FOLLOW ANY PREDETERMINED RULES OR STRUCTURE, SO NEWS CAN SPREAD RAPIDLY THROUGH IT.

Think of the grapevine as a piece of hardware, and the software is the stories that travel along the grapevine. While you can't control the grapevine, you can certainly influence it by the stories you proactively share and by your actions and decisions that generate stories. So it's worth understanding its power and how it works.

First of all, there are no formal rules governing the grapevine. Once a story is in the grapevine you will have no control over how many people it will reach or who it will reach.

There is also no quality control. Like Chinese whispers, the message can often be distorted. You will not know who heard the message or indeed what they actually heard.

It is not linear. The grapevine does not adhere to any top-down communication policy the company may have in place. There is also no control, no record of what is put into the grapevine and who put it in there. No-one needs any sign-off to put something into the grapevine. Which makes it superfast.

Poor decisions and inexcusable actions can lead to negative stories that in some cases can result in tremendous brand damage. Trust and reputation can be lost very quickly and can take a long time to recover.

STORIES CAN SPREAD QUICKLY, AND NEGATIVE STORIES TEND TO SPREAD MORE QUICKLY THAN POSITIVE ONES.

The good and the bad

In 2019 a group of private school boys from St Kevin's College in Melbourne were recorded singing sexist chants on public transport. That went viral and did tremendous brand damage to the school.

In 2020, mining giant Rio Tinto blasted caves in Western Australia's Pilbara region that they knew were of the highest archaeological significance in Australia. The cave sites were among the oldest in Australia, with evidence of continuous human habitation going back

46 000 years. They held high cultural significance for the traditional owners of the land, who were opposed to blasting the caves. Rio Tinto blew it up anyway and defended their actions — which again caused them tremendous brand damage.

Whenever I hear United Airlines, I think of them forcibly removing a passenger from their plane because they had overbooked the flight.

Whenever I hear Exxon, I think about the Exxon Valdez oil spill that occurred in 1989.

As the Exxon Valdez oil spill shows us, the grapevine can have a very long memory — which is not great if a negative story is circulating about you or your company. But if it's a positive story, then do your best to keep it alive.

For example, have you heard the story about the man who returned a set of tyres to a Nordstrom store? He bought them at a tyre shop, but the shop had since closed and a newly opened Nordstrom store was in its place. Nordstrom don't even sell tyres, but they still refunded the man's money in full.

There are so many blog posts and articles based on this story. If you search 'Nordstrom tires' you get over 7 110 000 references ... and it happened in 1975. That is 46 years ago, and people are still talking about it: decades of free publicity and word-of-mouth brand advertising.

THAT SINGLE ACT OF EXCEPTIONAL CUSTOMER SERVICE CREATED A BRAND STORY THAT HAS BEEN TOLD OVER AND OVER AGAIN.

I'm sure that the Nordstrom employee back in 1975 was not thinking about the longevity of the story; he was just living out Nordstrom's brand of providing exceptional customer service. If someone had told him that what he did would still be talked and written about decades later and it would have over 7 000 000 references on Google on the internet, he no doubt would have asked 'What is Google and what is the internet?'

I have researched the Nordstrom story extensively, and I can't find the original source. It's not clear if the customer or the company first communicated the story, hence putting it in the grapevine initially.

The key thing about the grapevine is, it's not the action that makes it into the grapevine; it's the *story that is created about the action*. If the customer doesn't tell anyone, if the employee doesn't tell anyone, if other customers or employees don't witness it and therefore don't tell anyone, then it goes unheard. No-one knows about it. No-one ever knows about it.

If the action results in a story being created, it goes into the grapevine; if there's no story it goes into oblivion.

In a world of social media, your customers will put most of these stories in the grapevine ... the positive and the negative. But you don't want to solely rely on your customers sharing stories for you.

Imagine if one of your employees did something like the Nordstrom employee and the customer never told anyone. What a missed opportunity to reinforce your brand.

Now I'm not suggesting that you put out a press release every time one of your employees delivers great customer service. But perhaps there are some stories that are worth sharing.

All the channels explored in the last chapter will put the stories into the grapevine and, if there is an attraction, people will start talking about it and sharing it. The Archie Rose gin distillery we discussed previously is a great example of this. The company put the story out there that they were swapping production of gin to hand sanitiser, and it spread like wildfire. People were attracted to the story.

Not all stories need to be shared on the external grapevine; your organisation has an internal grapevine that every single employee is part of every day.

This brings in the cyclic nature of the model I introduced at the start of this section. A brilliant customer experience story that is created by one of your employees' actions can be collected (added to the Greatest Hits album) and then communicated via any of the channels we discussed previously. Perhaps it becomes part the induction training or is shared in a newsletter, or simply in an email to your team.

THIS IS THE SPIRAL EFFECT OF BRAND STORYTELLING — IT'S THE ONGOING PROCESS OF COLLECTING, COMMUNICATING AND CREATING MORE AND MORE STORIES THAT SHOW YOUR BRAND IN ACTION.

I should mention that this is not a publicity stunt or marketing spin. People have a pretty good idea when something feels false. What you say and what you do need to be congruent with your brand. Your actions need to be aligned with your core values and purpose.

Some people will refer to it internally as 'optics',[1] meaning something will or won't look good for us. But whatever you call it, it's still talking about brand alignment. This is why defining your brand is such an important first step of brand storytelling.

Amplify your brand

How you react in a crisis can amplify your stories. We saw many examples of actions generating stories during the global coronavirus pandemic, from banks delaying mortgage payments to large corporates putting a freeze on all redundancies.

Such was the scrutiny that there was even a website that rated the actions of companies and celebrities during the pandemic. Called DidTheyHelp.com and founded and run by a group of volunteers across the globe, the site would rate the actions of companies and celebrities, categorising them as heroes or zeroes.[2]

For example, Airbnb were rated as heroes for providing free housing for first responders dealing with the COVID-19 outbreak when they asked hosts to donate rentals. They also said they would pay hosts $250 million to help cover cancellations due to COVID-19, and the founders took no salary for six months while top executives took a 50 per cent cut to help pay employees.

---

[1] Along with 'pivot', one of the most overused jargon words.
[2] By June 2020 they had added heroes or zeroes ratings to how companies and celebrities were responding to Black Lives Matter and LGBTQ rights.

Airbnb's authenticity

With travel restricted, Airbnb co-founder and CEO Brian Chesky sent a note to all Airbnb employees on 5 May 2020. It was widely circulated on social media with resoundingly positive comments on how heartfelt and authentic it was.

He confirmed the layoffs, saying:

> *Today, I must confirm that we are reducing the size of the Airbnb workforce. For a company like us whose mission is centered around belonging, this is incredibly difficult to confront, and it will be even harder for those who have to leave Airbnb.*

He then outlined how leadership came to the decision to let go of 25 per cent of employees, stating the guiding principles they used to decide on the reductions in the workforce, showing great transparency. He then went on to outline the specifics of how they would be taken care of, including severance details and job support. He ended with this:

> *Some final words. I have a deep feeling of love for all of you. Our mission is not merely about travel. When we started Airbnb, our original tagline was, 'Travel like a human.' The human part was always more important than the travel part. What we are about is belonging, and at the center of belonging is love.*
>
> *To those of you staying,*
>
> *One of the most important ways we can honor those who are leaving is for them to know that their contributions mattered, and that they will always be part of Airbnb's story. I am confident their work will live on, just like this mission will live on.*
>
> *To those leaving Airbnb,*
>
> *I am truly sorry. Please know this is not your fault. The world will never stop seeking the qualities and talents that you brought to Airbnb ... that helped make Airbnb. I want to thank you, from the bottom of my heart, for sharing them with us.*
>
> *Brian*

This email and the subsequent actions outlined in the email demonstrated their core values and helped generate positive stories on the grapevine.

CONGRATULATIONS! You did it! You're going places!

Another great example of how your actions create stories comes from my friend and fellow John Wiley & Sons author Margie Warrell.

During September 2020, Margie and her husband had to spend the mandatory 14 days in hotel quarantine when they arrived in Singapore after travelling from the United States. Like everyone else they had no choice of hotel, but they found themselves at the JW Marriott in Singapore. Margie said she 'couldn't have been happier' about where they landed because she had a bit of a history with Marriott hotels. A few years earlier she had run leadership programs with them as well as facilitating a 'fireside chat' with Mr Bill Marriott.

The flat rate set by the Singapore government for their two-week 'quarantine-staycation' was significantly less than the standard rate, particularly since they were upgraded to a suite when Margie enquired about the possibility of extra space as her and her husband both had to work. She had no expectations, so was extremely grateful for the upgrade.

You might reasonably have expected that the service standards would be lowered in such situations. However Margie said she experienced just the opposite: they were made to feel special throughout their entire stay. On the morning of their departure a gift was sitting on the chair outside their door: a congratulations certificate that read CONGRATULATIONS! You did it! You're going places!

Margie said she felt so special for doing nothing but not stepping outside their hotel room. The staff had no idea Margie was a best-selling author. They made her feel special, like everyone else no doubt felt special when they received their own congratulations certificate. Like Margie, they probably shared that with their family and friends. Some may have even posted a photo of their certificate on Facebook or Instagram, sharing the story of their experience even more widely.

Margie, however, being the author that she is, wrote an article about it that was published in *Forbes* magazine. She also recorded a video on the experience that she posted to her substantial number of followers.

The employees at JW Marriott did something that created a story ... that in this case was spread much wider than they ever would have dreamed about.

OUR ACTIONS CREATE IMMEDIATE STORIES, BUT SOMETIMES THE STORIES STILL HAVE CURRENCY YEARS AND YEARS LATER.

For example, the story of the CEO of Woolworths, Roger Corbett, returning the shopping trolley, Steve Jobs dropping the iPod in a fish tank and the Nordstrom employee refunding tyres.

So, to reiterate, you can't control the grapevine, but you can certainly influence it. Remember, if the grapevine is a piece of hardware, stories are the software. Stories are what fuel the grapevine.

There are already stories about your company swirling around the grapevine. But do you know what they are? Are you actively trying to influence the stories that are being shared?

ONCE YOU UNDERSTAND THE POWER OF THE GRAPEVINE AND IMPLEMENT BRAND STORYTELLING AS OUTLINED HERE, THEN YOU CAN START TO TAKE GREATER CONTROL OF YOUR BRAND AND AUTHENTICALLY CONNECT AND ENGAGE BOTH CUSTOMERS AND EMPLOYEES.

Check and reflect

- What stories are you creating?

- What stories are your employees creating every single day with every single customer transaction?

- Are they attracting people to your brand or repelling them against it?

- Are you looking for ways to create magnetic brand stories?

PART IV

see magnetic stories in ACTION

In research for this book, I interviewed lots of people to get diverse examples of stories told well, many of which you have read in the previous pages.

There were some companies, however, that really stood out with the way they are using brand storytelling strategically to communicate, both internally and externally. I decided that what these companies were doing could provide valuable insight to others.

What I found is explored in the following case stories. I have decided to call these 'case stories' instead of 'case studies' because I think that better reflects how they have been written.

Case studies don't have to be all factual information, which is normally how they are written. If you bring in more of the *people* as opposed to the process and results, it makes for a more engaging read.

I have also attempted to get some diversity in industry, size of company and location. From Mekong Capital, an investment company in Vietnam, to a fifth-generation family-owned bakehouse in Melbourne; an electricity provider in New Zealand to The Fullerton Hotels and Resorts from Singapore; and another fifth-generation family-owned business (but this one a restaurant in Florida).

My aim is that by providing more detail on how these companies implemented brand storytelling, and in sharing their specific stories, you will not only be inspired to do something similar, but gain some practical ways on how to go about doing it.

Even if you don't implement brand storytelling, I hope you find the stories in the following chapters as engaging and interesting as I do. It's also worth noting if you start to become connected to their brand through their stories. I can tell you one thing: the next time I am in Singapore, I will certainly be staying in the historic Fullerton Hotel Singapore, and the next time I'm in Florida I'll be making a beeline to the Columbia Restaurant. I already know what I'm going to order.

CASE STORY
Ferguson Plarre Bakehouses, Australia

Ferguson Plarre Bakehouses is a joint family-owned and -operated business in Australia. The Ferguson Plarre history commenced in 1901 in the northern and western suburbs of Melbourne as both families separately established themselves as household names. (Growing up in Melbourne, a pie or vanilla slice from either was always a special treat.)

The families continued trading through both World Wars and the Great Depression, despite the tough conditions. After years of friendly competition, the families merged their businesses to become Ferguson Plarre Bakehouses in 1980. The fourth generation of the Plarre family bought out the Ferguson family in 2012, but kept the well-known name. They still have a very strong brand, with 80 bakehouses across Melbourne. When my mother-in-law promises to bring a cake for dessert but runs out of time to bake one herself, it will always be from Ferguson's.

The CEO is Steve Plarre, who is fourth generation. He runs the company with his brother Mike, who is the General Manager of Manufacturing. Steve lives in Melbourne with his wife, Kate, and two young daughters, Elizabeth and Felicity. He loves to cook and loves exercising, especially running ... which is probably a good thing, being surrounded by pastry all day.

Karaoke cakes

Steve came to my attention in May 2020 during the lockdown restrictions of the coronavirus. I saw one of his 'Corona-oke' videos where he was singing and dancing to songs that he had changed the lyrics to. The first one I saw was a parody of the Queen classic 'I want to break free': here was a CEO dressed in drag like Freddie Mercury in the famous video clip, and changing the lyrics to 'I want to bake free'. (You can find the video on YouTube and the Ferguson Plarre Facebook page.)

My first thought was 'You don't see too many CEOs doing that'. With my interest piqued, I did a bit of digging around and found a recent interview where Steve explained why he started doing the videos. Basically, he said that their company purpose is 'To bring happiness to people through amazing experiences' and if they couldn't do it their normal way, with a sausage roll or vanilla slice, then maybe they could do it through a bit of karaoke fun.

Some of his other Corona-oke parodies were:

- 'Vanilla slice slice baby'

- 'We built this city on sausage rolls'

- 'Another one bites the crust'.

I contacted Steve and asked if I could have a chat to him about all things brand and storytelling. To my delight he said yes, and we spoke a few days later.[1]

I was impressed by Ferguson Plarre's understanding of the power of storytelling and experimentation with a variety of different forms. Storytelling seemed to be part of the way they communicated. Before I spoke to Steve, I was not even going to have case stories in this book, but they had so many good things to share that I decided a case story was in order.

---

[1] I also interviewed Steve for my Authentic Leadership podcast series, and you can find it at my website or through iTunes or SoundCloud.

Passion for the past

Steve told me that way back in 1997 they had produced a coffee table–style book. It was 100 pages full of pictures and stories that communicated the history of the two families.

The importance of history to the company became clear to me when, during our interview, I asked Steve to tell me a little bit about himself and the family business — and he immediately started to share the story of his great grandfather Otto, who was born in Germany and moved to Melbourne to open up a bakery. While it's a story I know he has told many times before, none of the passion has gone.

Otto grew up in a poor household with his parents and grandparents. His father was a cooper (beer barrel maker), so Otto was the first of the Plarre pastry cooks. Back in those days, dessert was a luxury reserved for the end of the week when or if there was food or money left over for something special. Living frugally back then meant that, for Otto, the real joy of cake came not so much from the ingredients but the fact that he could share it at the end of a long, hard day with his family.

Steve can only assume that at some stage Otto took such enjoyment from being served a meal and dessert with love by his family that it was a feeling he wanted to replicate for others, making it his career. All of this can only be assumed, but Steve has grown up in a household and inside a business where it's clear that the joy they get from running their business is inextricably linked to the happiness they create for others.

Steve acknowledges that you physically don't need a pie or cake to get through the day ... but, emotionally, a great-quality baked treat can bring you that little dash of sunshine! He uses the story of the Plarre family to make sure the staff all understand that it's all about the experience ... great food served with love and passion.

Steve says that Otto's story is 'easy to consume' and 'is real, authentic and memorable'. And this is what draws him to using stories as a way to communicate. The story of Otto Plarre, as well as the founding members of Ferguson's, are all on their website.

Steve makes sure that every Ferguson Plarre franchisee knows that

for every dollar that a customer gives you, 50 cents is for the product — and we'll make that as well as we can — but the other 50 cents is for how you make them feel … and if customers don't get a return on that second 50 cents, it doesn't matter how good the product is!

He doesn't want anyone to forget the origins of the family business, and he doesn't want to forget it either.

SHARING THE STORY HELPS GROUND HIM AND REMINDS HIM OF THE PASSION.

Defining their brand

When we map what the company has done well against the model outlined in the previous chapters, it's clear they have placed a strong focus on defining their brand. They know exactly what they want their brand to be.

They use a very simple one-pager that they call their 'brand temple'. It's a three-by-three matrix, depicting nine rooms with an overarching roof over the top that states 'Baking People Happy'.

There is real consistency across the rooms. The 'purpose room' declares the company purpose is 'to bring happiness to people through amazing experiences'. A similar room is the 'cause room' which says, 'Help simplify my life and give me little moments of joy'.

This is why the Corona-oke videos were so on brand. They ticked off the purpose (bring happiness) and the cause (little moments of joy). They also encapsulated a lot of the other values such as fun-loving, optimistic and relatable. Tick. Tick. Tick. Courageous. That is a very big tick. It is even congruent with their 'One family' value, as Steve features his two young daughters in some of the clips and his wife, Kate, who has a background in media and web content, even edits the videos.

They are also genuine. Steve plays in a band and writes songs, but he's not trying to launch his singing career through these videos. He is light-hearted with them but throws himself 100 per cent into it and pulls out some killer dance moves. You sort of get the feeling that he would be dancing around the house singing these songs regardless. There is real, genuine passion, and I admire him for that. (Even though he has destroyed how I'll listen to those Queen songs forever. He's even destroyed my love of Cindy Lauper's song 'Girls just want to have fun' by changing the lyrics to 'Girls just want to have buns' ... but I will forgive him for that.)

THE CRITICAL TAKEAWAY WE CAN GET FROM THIS IS THAT YOU NEED TO BE REALLY CLEAR ON WHAT YOUR BRAND IS, AND THEN STRATEGICALLY DO THINGS THAT ALIGN WITH THAT.

There has to be congruence in what you say and what you do.

Experiment with how to share stories

Once clear on their brand, the company experimented with a variety of ways to share stories. Their stores feature historical pictures on the walls. They include images of the owners across the generations, the old horse-drawn delivery carts and original stores. It even includes a copy of Otto's apprenticeship papers and a reference from his boss.

They also had a mural commissioned. With the use of mostly cartoon pictures and a few sentences, the mural manages to tell the story of the company. You could even call it a type of infographic.

The effectiveness of this mural lies in the fact that they didn't go about re-creating the entire timeline that's on their website. They didn't include everything. Steve said they included 'the things we talk about the most and are most proud of. We also chose the stories that we think are most relevant and relatable for our guests.'[2]

I counted the words on this mural, and in total there are only 168. But with the use of a few words and cartoon pictures, they really do communicate a lot.

---

[2] Notice Steve's use of the word 'guests' instead of 'customers'.

Maybe a vignette will do

They include micro stories or vignettes on their coffee cups, embracing the concept that lots of little stories make up your brand. Some might call them 'fun facts', but I think they add a bit more than just facts; I've decided to call them micro stories.

In 2016 the company was celebrating 115 years. They decided to include several micro stories on their takeaway cups. These included:

- 1901 — How long have we been baking? Put it this way, our first delivery trucks were powered by hay!

- 1925 — Ray Plarre was caned for designing cakes in maths class. Ray's pain was our gain!

- 1929 — The Great Depression hits. It stretched the dough but we are still here!

- 1935 — A sad year. Fire decimates our bakehouse in Brunswick. Thousands of pies lose their lives!

- 1963 — The Queen visits. Who bakes her sweet treats? You guessed it. Our goodies are fit for a Queen!

- 1966 — The President of the United States asks Ray Plarre to bake his cakes. American–Australian relations get a lot sweeter!

I laughed out loud when I read the one about thousands of pies losing their lives.

They embrace the concept of stories in other ways also, featuring videos about their franchisees on their website. In these videos the franchisees share personal stories of why they joined.

Who knows what 'axioms' mean?

Steve often shares stories at their gala awards. Steve says, 'The stories are for everyone. It's mostly me trying to use genuine family stories and attaching them to our "Baking People Happy" message.' Steve added that for him, 'It's always about trying to use real stories to connect back to our brand because real stories are easier to remember and become undeniable axioms of truth.' I love his insight into 'axioms of truth'. I'm going to be really honest here: I had to look up what axioms meant. According to the Collins dictionary, an axiom 'is a statement or idea which people accept as being true'. This goes back to what my favourite corporate anthropologist, Michael Henderson, was saying: that stories can transcend truth.

These stories are also shared as part of the induction process. Every employee and franchisee is scheduled to spend 30 minutes with Steve to be taken through the family history. Steve tells them the founder story about Otto around the dinner table and how the Ferguson Plarre business did not start in the 1900s when Otto first opened his bakery doors ... it started as a spark of gratitude in his mind when he was eating with his family in Germany.

A story by any other name ...

One final aspect worth mentioning with Ferguson Plarre Bakehouses is what they call things on their website. If you go to their website, you will see they have not replaced the 'About Us' section with 'Our Story' as so many companies do.

What they have is an 'About Us' section that provides a brief description about the company. They then have an 'Our History' section. While this is in date order like any timeline, it's written in a way that is more engaging than typical timelines. It includes little stories as well as the significant events that happened in that year. It's a great example of how you could do a timeline.

They also have separate sections sharing the history behind some of their most popular and iconic products, including the history of the meat pie, lamingtons and Tiddly Oggies ... which I had never heard of but is what they call their Cornish pasties because 'tiddly oggie' is Cornish for 'proper pastry'.

They even share the history of their Not Cross Buns, which don't have a cross on them but rather a smiley face. The Not Cross Bun was first created in 2014, solely to bring attention to the fact that major grocery retailers were selling hot cross buns on Boxing Day. Their creation formed a key part of Ferguson Plarre Bakehouses' push to keep Easter special by limiting the sale of hot cross buns to the six weeks before Easter.

They are calling sections on their website what they are: not calling their timeline a 'story', not calling their 'About Us' a story, not calling their history of lamingtons a 'story'. You actually don't see the word 'story' on their website, yet they share a lot of stories.

IMPLEMENTING STORYTELLING AS A WAY TO COMMUNICATE YOUR BRAND IS NOT ABOUT TALKING ABOUT THE WORD 'STORY' — IT'S ABOUT SHARING ACTUAL STORIES.

Check and reflect

- Are there creation stories about your business that every new employee should know about?

- Who should share those stories?

- Is your company at the size that the CEO could dedicate individual time to each employee?

- If it's too large for that to happen one on one, how else could you replicate that?

- Could you do something that has nothing to do with selling your products but is still on brand? (Karaoke is not for everyone, but what else could you do?)

- Could you use micro stories in a fun way, like they did with the coffee cups?

- How else could you experiment with sharing and generating stories?

CASE STORY
Columbia Restaurant, Florida, USA

Columbia Restaurant is Florida's oldest restaurant, and the largest Spanish restaurant in the world. It was founded in 1905 by a Cuban immigrant, Casimiro Hernandez Sr.

I was first alerted to Columbia's use of stories by my friend Denise Collazo, who dined at the Florida restaurant and noticed they used stories on the menu. (Stories on the menu? That really got my attention!) So, considering the Florida restaurant is a lazy 24-hour-plus flight from my home in Melbourne, I checked out their website instead.

Their stories were indeed all over their menus, as well as scattered throughout the various sections of their website.

Let's start with the stories on the menu, which highlight that stories don't need to be long for you to create a connection with them. Here are a few examples (and apologies in advance if it makes you hungry).

Spanish Bean Soup

The soup that made the Columbia famous. The original recipe of Casimiro Hernandez, Sr: garbanzo beans simmered with smoked ham, chorizo sausage and potatoes in a delicious broth of chicken and ham.

Picadillo 'Criollo'

We could always count on enjoying our mother and grandmother Adela Hernandez Gonzmart's delicious picadillo recipe at her home. A family favorite for generations. Finely ground choice lean beef, braised with onions, green peppers, olives, raisins and capers. Served with white rice and ripe platanos.

Crab Enchilado

A Sunday favorite when we were children. A mildly spicy sauce of fresh lump blue crabmeat, tomatoes, onions, green peppers, garlic, oregano, and white wine. Served over pasta.

My favourites, however, came from the wines listed on the menu. (Again, apologies in advance if this makes you feel like a drink.)[1]

AG Rosado 100% Tempranillo Rosé

Selected by Richard Gonzmart as a surprise for his daughter, from Rioja, Spain.

Rusty Red

Rusty is the creation of Richard Gonzmart as a tribute to the unconditional love between a man and his dog. 100% Tempranillo red wine from Rioja, Spain.

Enzi Chardonnay

Created in memory of 5th-generation family member Andrea Gonzmart's beloved German Shepherd, Enzi, who lost her battle with cancer. Napa Valley, CA.

And, talking about wine: they have an extensive 224-page wine list that reads more like a storybook than a wine list. They share a short story of each winery they purchase wine from, and another story about the wine maker.

---

[1] I was writing this at 9 am and it made me feel like a drink.

Is your story a Netflix series?

The history page on their website is also written as such an engaging story that it could easily be the script of a movie. Here are just the few opening paragraphs:

It began in Tampa's Ybor City, (pronounced EE-bore) as a small 60-seat corner café known for its Cuban coffee and authentic Cuban sandwiches, frequented by the local cigar workers.

As the Prohibition movement gained steam, Casimiro Sr. faced a bitter dilemma. He could lose his saloon or find a new use for the Columbia. He did not have to look far. Manuel Garcia, who owned La Fonda, the restaurant next door, agreed in 1919 to join him and retain the name 'Columbia.' The size of the Columbia doubled overnight. Also, in 1919, his son, Casimiro Hernandez Jr., joined the business. Following the death of Casimiro Sr. in 1929, Casimiro Jr. took over ownership and operation of the restaurant.

Casimiro Jr. aspired to take the Columbia beyond its humble beginnings and envisioned an elegant dining room with music and dancing, the likes of which were unheard of in this part of the country at the time. During the height of the Depression in 1935, he took a chance by building the first air-conditioned dining room in Tampa, complete with an elevated dance floor. He named it the Don Quixote Room.

Casimiro Jr. and his wife, Carmen, had one child, Adela Hernandez Gonzmart. Adela was a concert pianist who was trained at the Juilliard School of Music. In 1946, Adela married Cesar Gonzmart, a concert violinist. They traveled throughout the United States while Cesar performed in famous supper clubs during the early 1950s. In 1953, Adela's father, Casimiro Jr., was in failing health, so they returned to Tampa. They divided the business duties of operating the restaurant and raising their two sons, Casey and Richard.

The family persevered in keeping the restaurant open during the late 1950s and all through the 1960s when Ybor City was dying. Many of the row houses that once housed the cigar workers had decayed into slums. Urban renewal cut the heart from the Latin Quarter. More families moved out. Businesses closed. Cesar Gonzmart realized they had to do something to bring people back to Ybor City ...

Your stories can create real suspense and intrigue about your company — cliffhanger endings that makes you want to know more.[2]

Long-term commitment to collecting

I contacted Marketing and Public Relations Manager Jeff Houck, who has been working with the company since 2015.

I wanted to ask Jeff when the company made the decision to use stories so heavily. I got the feeling it wasn't a couple of years ago, but maybe it was about ten years ago, when storytelling was starting to gain some traction in the business world as a legitimate way to communicate. His answer blew me away.

This decision was made in 1946. They hired a newspaper journalist called Paul Wilder who wrote a newspaper column five times a week, sharing recipes and specials and — most popular — stories, anecdotes, interviews and observations. They were actually paid advertisements, but, as Jeff said, 'Paul told the stories of the characters of the restaurant. It never was told as an advertisement.'

One such story comes from a column written by Paul in 1951:

A tall ruddy-faced stranger sat down in the Don Quixote court and ordered dinner. He was all by himself. He told the waitress, 'You know I am here tonight because of a dead man. I am a member of the Royal Northeast Mounted Police. I have been in it for 11 years. Eight years ago I was on duty in the Yukon Territory where I found a drowned man. I searched him for identification and among his papers was a card from the Columbia Restaurant in Tampa, Florida, with a picture of a statue and a fountain. For some strange reason, I kept the card ... I thought that

---

[2] Which of course you can at the history page of the Columbia Restaurant's website.

someday I would visit there.' As he left he said the picture of the Columbia was fulfilled and that he will be back again in three more years.

Jeff says the second- and third-generation owners 'really understood storytelling' and that today across their five restaurant brands they use stories extensively, stating that 'almost everything on the menu has a small bit of narrative' that he knows the customers connect with.

Showcasing customers

They also feature their customers in their stories. In fact, Jeff said, 'We do our best work when we share stories of the people that visit Columbia.'

For example, the story they shared on Valentine's Day in 2020 of a couple that have been coming to the restaurant on their wedding anniversary for 71 years. It read:

> *If you had to bestow a title of Sweethearts of the Columbia, Mits and Fannie Zamore of Tampa would be at the top of the lovebirds list.*
>
> *Each January, they celebrate their wedding anniversary at the Columbia in Ybor the same way they have for 71 years in a row: by sitting at the same table in the Patio dining room, No. 370.*
>
> *They've kept to their annual tradition of toasting to their love with a strawberry Pink Squirrel cocktail. The couple sat at this table the first year, then got the same table accidentally the next year. Then it became a seven-decade tradition.*
>
> *Columbia salutes the Zamores on their wonderful life together and wishes sweethearts everywhere a Valentine's Day full of love.*

Jeff told me that they are 'less interested in sharing stories about the food but rather the stories about their customers. In the process we show them choosing us, and that's an honour.'

The stories don't end with the history on the website, the origin of the food and wine on the menus and the loyal customers; they find opportunities to share stories on a variety of topics.

Heritage stories

On their website they share the stories of the various artworks and stained glass windows that adorn the restaurant.

There is a video on their YouTube channel about their iconic chandelier that was purchased in 1936 for £550 and is now worth US$250 000 ... and how the 1880 lights in it were painstakingly cleaned in 2018.

The YouTube channel also features other video stories, such as one following the journey of the bread from the 100-year-old bakery that they have been getting their bread from since the start, and the story of current president Richard Gonzmart's favourite table, where he first met his wife. (He never sits at that table with anyone but her.)

They actively look for opportunities to share stories. On 4 July 2019 they wrote on their Facebook page,

> On Fourth of July, we remember the patriotic origins of our name.
>
> In 1903, founder Casimiro Hernandez, Sr., named his new Ybor City café the Columbia Saloon out of gratefulness for his asylum in the land of opportunity.
>
> The saloon's name was inspired by the song 'Columbia, Gem of the Ocean,' a popular patriotic tune at the time which functioned as an unofficial national anthem in competition with 'Hail, Columbia' and 'The Star-Spangled Banner.'
>
> The name Columbia, in fact, served as a nickname for the United States of America in the 19th century.

Engaging employees

The second- and third-generation owners' commitment to storytelling has clearly continued to this day. Jeff explained that every person who comes and works in the Columbia Restaurant (about 1000 employees) learns about the stories as part of their induction. Every week they hold team meetings where another story is shared.

For their hundredth anniversary they produced a coffee table–style book called *The Columbia Book* and Jeff confessed that he read it about four times in his first few months. The stories are the basis of continuing education for all employees. Jeff said the motivation for employees to learn these stories is 'you don't want to be the waiter that knows less than your customer'.

They know that their staff being able to explain the story behind the chandelier, or the statue in the fountain, or where the recipe originates from, enhances the customer experience. As Jeff says, it

> *goes so far beyond the plate and the table. That, yes, people are spending money on their food, but, more importantly, they are voting with their time. We know that when we share stories it becomes an immersive emotional experience.*

Jeff sees it firsthand: customers come in and repeat these stories for friends that are visiting for the first time. They bring their friends from out of town and 'they reshare the stories with pride'. He reflected that 'if your customers love the stories they hear they will share them and become your story evangelists and your brand ambassadors'. This comment from Jeff is the essence of brand loyalty.

You need look no further than the Columbia Restaurant to see the proof that stories connect with customers and engage employees. They have over 1000 employees and, in an industry that is known for its high turnover, 28 per cent of their employees have a tenure longer than ten years.

It's interesting that all this information on their website is under a tab called 'The Columbian Experience', which I think is an appropriate name. Reading these stories I feel like I have experienced the restaurant without having actually been there.

I finished my conversation with Jeff with him telling me that they have kept the legacy of Paul Wilder alive: they know, by keeping records and recording information now, that it's all about 'future storytelling'.

When they reopened their restaurants in June 2020 after the coronavirus forced closures, they hung banners from their restaurant that simply read, 'We're open again — make some history with us.'

RECORDING AND SHARING STORIES FROM THE PAST AND THE PRESENT WILL HELP COMMUNICATE YOUR BRAND IN THE FUTURE.

Check and reflect

- How could you share stories about heirlooms or artefacts in your company that hold special value beyond monetary value, like Columbia Restaurant's chandelier, fountain or recipes?

- How could you share stories about rituals, like Richard only ever sitting at a particular table with his wife?

- Do your customer-facing employees know stories that can enhance the customer experience?

- Do you actively share stories of your customers?

- Do you actively encourage customers to share their stories and engage with them on social media when they do?

- Can you rewrite the timeline of your company so it's more like a Netflix series?

CASE STORY
The Fullerton Hotels and Resorts, Singapore (and Sydney)

In early 2020, I had the pleasure of staying at the newly opened Fullerton Hotel in Sydney. (Little did I know it would be the last time I stayed in a hotel for quite a long time due to the COVID-19 pandemic that took the world by storm in early 2020. If I had known, I really would have made the most of room service and the mini bar.)

It was on this trip, however, that I noticed a beautiful coffee table–style book on the display table as I was walking to my room. It was titled *Fullerton Stories — Rediscovering Singapore's Heritage*. Intrigued, I had a flick through it and took a photo of the cover to remind myself to look into it at some point.

Then about a week later, my professional world as I knew it, of travel, room service and eating Pringles from the mini bar, came to a dramatic stop. So, I didn't really do that exploring until I started writing this book and remembered the stories I read in Sydney.

If you don't know about The Fullerton Hotels and Resorts, their signature hotels are in Singapore and Sydney, and two of the iconic buildings are former General Post Offices which have been lovingly restored into five-star luxury hotels.

Cavaliere Giovanni Viterale is the General Manager of The Fullerton Hotels and Resorts and is based in Singapore. Giovanni told me, 'We are very fortunate to be able to take care of these historic national monuments, which contain countless stories and memories of people who have lived, worked and played in the historic buildings.'

In 2015, The Fullerton Hotel in Singapore was recognised as a national monument, representing the highest form of preservation and national recognition.

The Singapore building was not only where the post office was, but it also housed many other government departments, including the tax office, the import and export department, the finance ministry and the office of the chief health officer. Giovanni explained that 'in that building, decisions were made by Singapore pioneers that steered Singapore from a third world to a first world country'.

While the *Fullerton Stories* book was a great initiative, they didn't want history confined to 'only pictures in a book'; they wanted to 'bring the stories alive'.

They have also created a series of videos that feature people who used to work in the historic buildings. The videos, like the book, are called 'Fullerton Stories, rediscovering Singapore's heritage' and 'Rediscovering Sydney's heritage'.

Great personalities

To find these stories, they initially wrote to the respective government departments and asked for the archive records. They also put publicity posts on social media asking for people who used to work in the buildings to contact them. They were inundated with people wanting to be a part of this campaign to share their memories. Everyone was 'open and excited and we collected more than what we needed'.

Giovanni and the team at Fullerton call the people they chose to feature 'personalities' … which is a great description.

For example, the Singapore series includes personalities such as M Bala Subramanion, who started working at the post office in 1946 until his retirement in 1971. He proudly shows a photo of himself receiving a medal from the first President of Singapore, Yusof Ishak, and says it was the 'proudest moment of my life'.

And there is also the story of a couple that have been married for 53 years. They met in the General Post Office in the 1960s when they both worked as postal clerks. Robert Lim shares how he was attracted to this girl so he 'tried to be nice to her'. Tan Lat Neo, now spouse to Mr Robert Lim, recalled she was initially annoyed because she was distracted by his advances. But eventually she realised he 'had good intentions'.

The Sydney stories feature personalities such as Gloria Velleley and Gloria Cochrane, who worked as telephonists in the Sydney building. They share stories of people based in Antarctica calling home and, because they felt sorry for them, they would let them talk as long as possible without charging them. They recall that every shift they were rostered on to tell the time for half an hour: for 30 minutes, every ten seconds they would have to read out the time. Every. Ten. Seconds. On one shift Gloria Velleley said she had to do it for 45 minutes and 'nearly went bonkers'.

They share a story of cutting in on a phone call between a man and woman. The woman was trying to tell the man 'I love you'. Due to interference on the line he couldn't hear and kept saying 'say it again'. After the third time of the woman trying to get him to hear 'I love you', Gloria cut in and said 'I love you' to which the man replied, 'Thank you operator, I love you too.'

Another story featured Leslie Edwards, who started working in the building as a telegrapher in 1954, sending Morse code. He proudly holds a photograph taken on 13 December 1962, when the last Morse code message was sent. One of his colleagues, Harry Winchester, was retiring that day, so they gave him the honour of sending that last message. Leslie kept a photograph of Harry sending the message with all his colleagues looking on, including Leslie himself as a 24-year-old.

In one of the videos they interviewed the architect who oversaw the refurbishment of the building in Singapore, and he says, 'As an architect we want to respect what we have inherited.' I can't help but feel that they have done that, with not only the buildings, but with the stories of the people who worked in those buildings. They have truly appreciated what they inherited, and the value of stories as well as bricks and mortar.

At the official opening of The Fullerton Hotel Sydney, these videos were shown and the people featured in them were invited to the official opening.

The videos can be found on their website, YouTube channel and other social media sites. They form part of an interactive feature that also includes photographs and stories in a prominent position in the lobby of The Fullerton Hotel Singapore, called the heritage gallery.

The videos are also accessible on TV in all the guest rooms. One day they had some of the personalities at the hotel for afternoon tea when an English tourist walked past and recognised some of the personalities. She stopped and said with excitement, 'I just watched you on my TV.'

As part of keeping these stories alive, the Fullerton also runs complimentary heritage tours at the hotels. Many locals and international guests enjoy the tours.

Engaging and enhancing

Internally they also use the stories in other ways. The videos are used as part of their orientation program. Not only do all new employees watch the videos, they also go on the heritage tours and learn other key insights about the hotel, including history and stories. This happens in both the Singapore and Sydney hotels.

These stories are used to enhance the customer experience. For example, any server can explain to a guest the history behind the chicken rice they ordered and why this is an important dish to a specific region. This backs up what Kim Seagram from Tasmania shared about the importance of stories in enhancing the dining experience.

Another way they enhance the customer experience is by giving guests a postcard that they post through original colonial red postal pillar boxes installed in both The Fullerton Hotel in Singapore and the hotel in Sydney.

On their websites, under the tab appropriately named 'Our Heritage', it says 'Welcome to the Fullerton Heritage where history meets the future'. This is another great example of how a history timeline can be engaging by combining dates, facts and stories. You can view this in its entirety on their website, but here is just a snapshot.

11th century — Singapore, The Lion City

According to early Malay history, Singapura was founded in the 11th century by a mighty Srivijayan ruler, Sang Nila Utama, or Sri Tri Buana, Prince of Palembang. Sailing past the island of Temasek, the prince caught sight of a great lion standing guard at the mouth of the river. To the Srivijayans, the lion was the symbol of royalty and a powerful omen. Sri Tri Buana moved his royal court to the island and named his new capital Singapura, 'city of the Lion'.

In the late 14th century, the Javanese sent their mighty fleet to conquer the island. The Srivijayan palaces were destroyed and the inhabitants scattered.

In time the city disappeared beneath a verdant jungle cover. The only remains of the great city were the mighty ramparts, royal tombs, and a huge stone monument which marked the entrance to the city.

1819 — Raffles Landing

On 6th February 1819 Sir Stamford Raffles anchored off St John's Island and rowed in the Singapore River. Passing the rocky, high promontory which formed the entrance to the river, he wondered if this was indeed a mythical lion, standing guard over the ancient royal city.

At the tip of this promontory lay a large stone monument, inscribed with an ancient script. Raffles was certain he found the lost city of Singapura. He raised the British flag and restored the island to the name Singapore.

It then goes on to describe significant events, such as how a fortress was built in 1820 called Fort Fullerton, named after the first governor, Sir Robert Fullerton. It details how the Fullerton building was opened in 1928 and the independence of Singapore in 1965, through to the restoration and opening of the Fullerton Hotel in 2001.

In 2015, the Fullerton Hotel in Singapore was officially gazetted as a Singapore national monument by the country's National Heritage Board, ensuring the building will be preserved.

I love the fact that the closing credits of the videos make the claim that the hotels are 'A custodian of heritage'.

THE HISTORY AND HERITAGE OF THE COMPANY IS PRESERVED AND PROTECTED BY THESE STORIES.

Check and reflect

- Are there any stories worth sharing about who used to work in the building your company now operates from?

- Could you dedicate space in your building to share these stories?

- Do your customer-facing employees know stories they could share that could enhance the customer experience?

- Could you actively share stories of your customers?

- Could you share stories of the personalities that used to work in the building or for your company from years ago?

CASE STORY
Mekong Capital, Vietnam

Mekong Capital is based in Vietnam, with offices in Ho Chi Minh City and Hanoi. It's a private equity firm, and the companies they invest in are typically among the fastest growing market-leading companies in Vietnam.

It was established in 2001 by Chris Freund. Chris grew up in Chicago and is a massive fan of 1980s music. In his early twenties he did a year abroad studying Buddhism in India and living as a Buddhist monk in Thailand. After that he backpacked around the region, including a month in Vietnam.

Expecting a hostile and war-torn environment after watching movies such as *Apocalypse Now*, he was pleasantly surprised at how friendly everyone was in Vietnam. In 1994, he moved there for what was meant to be three years, but he never returned. He now calls Vietnam home, where he lives with his wife and two daughters.

In late 2007, Mekong Capital commenced an intensive transformation of its corporate culture. Two years later the positive impact of this transformation was clear, and, in 2010, Mekong Capital was the subject of case studies at the Harvard and London business schools. You know you are doing something right when these business schools want to showcase your work in a case study![1]

What do you value?

As part of this transformation they developed core values that guide the day-to-day decisions of everyone who works for the firm. They are the most unique core values I have come across in my entire career.

Seven of the eight core values are made-up words. They are:

1. *Resultership:* the combination of 'results' and 'leadership', which means holding themselves and others accountable to do whatever is necessary to produce results, but always in a way that is consistent with the other core values.

2. *Springthrough:* the combination of 'spring' and 'breakthrough', which is about inspiring themselves and others to step out of comfort zones, play a bigger game and choose empowering contexts, which lead to new actions and breakthrough results.

3. *Victorance:* the combination of 'victory' and 'perseverance', which means a fearless and relentless perseverance until the goal is achieved, regardless of whatever obstacles seem to be in the way.

4. *Beautegrity:* the combination of 'beauty' and 'integrity', which is about honouring their word so that everything works. It also means working together as a unified and powerful force.

5. *Communiplete:* the combination of 'communicate' and 'complete', which means communicating in a direct way so that nothing is misunderstood or unhandled.

6. *Inquisity:* the combination of 'inquisitive' and 'curiosity', which means to relentlessly pursue the root cause and key drivers behind

---

[1] If you're interested in reading the case studies you can find the Harvard Business School one at hsb.edu, 'Mekong Capital: Building A Culture of Leadership in Vietnam', and London Business School's by searching 'Mekong Capital: The importance of corporate culture in emerging market private equity'. This was also included in the textbook *International Private Equity* by Eli Talmor and Florin Vasvari.

events or trends, and pushing the boundaries in generating game-changing insights.

7. *Jeromosity:* the combination of 'generosity' and the name 'Jerome', who was Chris's mentor, which means to see the best in others and empower them.

8. *Genesis:* this is not a made-up word, and relates to being at the source of the actions they take, the impact they have and how the world materialises around them. For Mekong Capital, this word means being the cause rather than the effect.

Chris shared with me that the creation of new words was deliberate: they wanted to create a shared language and wanted each team member to personally discover the meaning of each core value without bringing their pre-existing assumptions. They know a potential problem with made-up words is that if they inadvertently use them with people outside the company, it can be confusing for them. They are therefore extremely disciplined in ensuring they do not use these internal terms with outsiders unless they explain them.

Having the core values written this way even encourages guests to their head office to ask about what they mean, giving them an opportunity to discuss their values. This was a surprising result to Chris, but an opportunity the team love. Think about the last time you walked into a corporate office and saw the standard values of integrity, respect, innovation—can you imagine asking them what they meant?

A framework to follow

They also developed what they called a 'Vision Driven Investment' framework. This framework evolved over the years and consists of 14 principles that they call 'elements'. It's a framework they use to support and grow the companies they invest in.

Chris said that when they invest in companies it's under the premise that they will adopt the Vision Driven Investment framework. When Mekong Capital invest in companies, they work with them to implement the 14 elements that make up this framework, since they had achieved great success adopting the elements themselves and they had seen similar success when companies they invested in also adopted them.

The 14 elements in the framework include:

- creating a clear vision for their future

- building a strong management team and corporate culture necessary for achieving their vision

- using data analytics to make well-informed decisions and optimise performance.

When Chris contacted me after recently reading my book *Stories for Work*, he had an audacious goal to find and document 100 stories over a 12-month period, stories they could use to communicate and demonstrate their eight core values and the 14 guiding elements that made up the Vision Driven Investment framework. Chris knew these stories would be helpful immediately, but the end game for Chris and the team was to publish a book containing all these stories that would help any company be successful.

I love a good vision and challenge, and I was excited that Chris asked me to be part of their journey. So, we followed the Implementing Brand Storytelling framework outlined in Part III of define, teach, collect, communicate and create.

Chris and the team had a very clear purpose of what they wanted to achieve. They had clarity around the culture they wanted to implement and be known for, and their eight core values. Plus, they had identified the 14 elements that they had adopted and shared with the companies they invested in.

When they started the process of gathering stories, they were very clear that they wanted stories around the eight core values and the 14 elements.

Chris saw the value in skilling up his team on how to share these stories more effectively, hence his contact with me. In March 2018 I travelled to Ho Chi Minh City to spend three days with Chris and the team of about 15 people.

Most of my clients invest half a day to educate the relevant people on how to share stories better. Some do a full day to start the process of finding stories. I was impressed by their commitment to spend three days on this. We went through all the aspects of storytelling that I shared in the 'teach' section of part III.

I can still recall the sight of the boardroom. One wall consisted of a large built-in whiteboard where we listed the eight core values and 14 elements. As stories were shared amongst the team they were added to the list. It was easier to find stories to demonstrate some of the core values or elements than others. At the end of the three days they were well on their way, having identified over 60 stories they could share. This was an amazing effort when the goal was 100 for the year.

One aspect of the training was that each team member would share a story about one of the 14 elements. This served two purposes. First, it was an opportunity for them to practise the stories and get feedback from me and the rest of the team. Second, it was the start of the collect process. The story sharing had started. And because they were now educated in not only the power of storytelling but how to share stories more effectively, they were identifying where and when they could share these stories. I remember after one story was shared another team member said, 'That is a perfect story I could use with a current client who is not seeing the value in creating a vision.' We would then get this second team member to reshare the story, which was another way to practise the story and get feedback.

This was beneficial for the people in the room who heard all these stories—but they wanted to share them more broadly and ensure they weren't forgotten. Remember, the end game was to use these stories as part of the book they would publish. They decided that all these initial stories should be written up.

Systemising success

In a great example of how fast a company can move, overnight one of the team set up a database for the stories to be stored in their internal system, Confluence. It was a great system that allowed people to add their story to the respective value or element. This way gaps were easily identified.

The other great feature of this database was that some people had access to edit the stories. Finally, people could also provide feedback and vote, which gave great insights into what stories were really resonating with people.

THE TEAM WERE SO COMMITTED TO FINDING STORIES THAT THEY AGREED TO MAKE FINDING AND DOCUMENTING STORIES IN THE DATABASE A PART OF THEIR MONTHLY AND QUARTERLY KEY PERFORMANCE INDICATORS.

They still have those key performance indicators today, so the number of stories keeps growing.

The team also implemented a process to keep the momentum of finding and sharing stories going. Once a month they would hold a story-sharing session that anyone in the organisation could attend. This allowed people to practise sharing stories, but also to actually share them with all employees. These could be their own personal stories around the core values, or stories of their colleagues living the core values, as well as stories about the 14 elements, which could be about what they were doing internally or what their partners were doing.

Two years after commencing this work and at the time of writing this book they had well over 400 stories documented in their internal system.

Prioritise your audience and stories

When it came to communicating stories, there were four distinct target audiences identified. These were, in order of priority:

1. employees

2. invested companies

3. potential investors

4. general public.

CHRIS SAID THAT THE HIGHEST PRIORITY WAS TO SHARE STORIES INTERNALLY WITH THEIR EMPLOYEES, TO ENGAGE THEM IN THE VALUES AND CULTURE AND RAISE THE INSTITUTIONAL KNOWLEDGE OF WHAT WORKED BEST, OR DIDN'T WORK, IN MEKONG'S HISTORY.

Internally they share the stories with employees in a variety of situations. Maybe a team meeting, perhaps a one-on-one coaching session, and as part of their induction program. All stories are documented in their internal system, and employees are encouraged to read them as more and more stories get added.

The purpose of sharing stories around company values is to ensure they are fully understood and that people connect and engage with them. It's very hard to communicate stories through bullet points.

When most companies 'roll out' new values they state the value and then have a few bullet points underneath to explain what that means. Which is neither engaging nor effective. There is a very good reason why this book is not called 'Magnetic Bullet Points'. If I wanted to write a book on the effectiveness of bullet points it would be called 'Teflon Bullet Points' ... which would be more accurate.

In action!

From the very first moment I started working with the team at Mekong Capital, it was evident that they were living and breathing their values. These were not espoused values; these were values in action. I want to share two moments that demonstrate this.

The first was on the first day of the training. I arrived early to set up the room to start at our scheduled time, 9 am. At a few minutes before 9 am, every single person was in the room waiting to start the training. This is the only time I have experienced this ... well, the only time I can remember. I was so impressed that I made a mention of thanking everyone for being there on time. I received a few confused looks before Chris explained, 'Integrity is part of our values, which means honouring your word, so if you say you will be at a meeting at 9 ... you will be at a meeting at 9.'[2]

Another example came towards the end of the three days where we debriefed. One of the senior team members spoke up, saying he needed to apologise to me. I was confused—I had no idea what he was talking about. He said to me that after day one he thought it was a waste of time to have everyone practise their stories and he told some of the team

---

[2] This is a far cry from a lot of people who run late for meetings. You know the ones: they apologise for being late, blaming something, but still have time to stop and grab a takeaway latte ... I call this running latte.

members this. But he could now see the huge benefit in this, to not only practise but to start the process of sharing and collecting the stories. He then went on to say, 'In the spirit of our value Communiplete, which means to communicate in a direct way so that nothing is misunderstood, I wanted to let you know that myself.'

These are only two examples of many I could share with you. The employees in Mekong were so attuned to what the values meant that they not only talked about them, but their actions demonstrated them. They would call each other and, more importantly, themselves out when they felt values and actions were not aligned.

Chris said while it's hard to measure the success of using stories, he knows that 'the pace of people stepping up and being more independent doing their jobs is clear'.

Their second priority is to share stories with the companies they invest in, which they refer to as partners. Chris explained, 'We use the stories from our other partners to inspire our new partners with what is possible.'

He provided an example of one partner that was reluctant to implement the Agile framework. It was only through sharing stories of the success another partner had with Agile that they got on board with it.

These stories are normally in relation to the 14 elements to help educate their business partners about what is possible, as well as providing valuable content on how to implement the Vision Driven Investment elements. So sometimes they cross over into case studies where they explain processes and communicate results—but they still stay true to the engaging nature of storytelling. They move beyond case studies to not only show them the how but also inspire them and show them why. Something I call a case story.

This is a great example of how stories and case studies can work in conjunction with each other.

STORIES CAN BE USED TO INFLUENCE AND EXCITE PEOPLE, WHICH IS THEN FOLLOWED BY THE CASE STUDY TO SHOW THEM HOW TO DO IT.

The third priority is to share their stories with potential investors. If there is a time when you want to really connect, engage and influence, it's when you are talking to potential investors.

In the past they would run information sessions for potential investors that would be very much in the PowerPoint presentation style, with facts and figures. But Chris advised that once they started to realise the power of storytelling they completely changed the format to be focused around stories.

Now they have their senior leaders plus the deal leaders and a couple of more junior staff in the room. Between them they share about a dozen relevant stories. Chris informed me that the potential investors 'love it' and that stories are a big part of making the session more engaging.

Chris also shares a story of a failed investment with them. He believes this transparency is important. Chris said that they have always been transparent, but this particular story of failure 'is pushing the envelope because it almost makes us look incompetent'. He went on, 'The fact that we are sharing it and committed to learning from it shows that we are not making the same mistake again, and the reaction is always positive.'

During the coronavirus restrictions they had to run these sessions virtually, so I had the opportunity to attend one. The session was literally called 'Story Sharing', and that is exactly what they did. They explained to their audience, the potential investors, their commitment to communicating through stories. Over the next 90 minutes they shared eight stories, providing time for people to ask questions at the end of each story.

Chris started the session by sharing his story about their worst ever failed investment, but throughout the story he detailed the key lessons they had learnt because of that. I witnessed firsthand that Chris sharing this story of failure showed that they were transparent and, more importantly, had learnt valuable lessons that had not been repeated.

The final priority is sharing stories with the general public. A selection of those current 400-plus documented stories are shared externally on social media platforms such as Facebook, LinkedIn, Medium and Quora. Chris believes the main benefit of this is for recruitment to attract talented people. He wants potential employees who are excited to be a part of Mekong Capital's culture, who understand the values and therefore expected behaviours before they join the firm.

Chris reflected that he is surprised how many people read these stories on social media and their mailouts:

> *I get a lot of people going out of their way to mention that they liked reading the story. It helps build awareness of what Mekong is about and they are all about the core values so they experience what the culture is like.*

One final word from Chris. When I asked him about the overall impact of making that decision to communicate their key messages both internally and externally through stories, he said, 'It's been a huge success— I recognise this initiative to be very effective and it just keeps building.'

Check and reflect

- How could you include stories in your stakeholder engagement meetings?

- How could you share stories about your employees on your professional (and maybe personal) social media sites?

- How well are your values understood (really understood) so they influence actions and are spoken about on a daily basis?

- Regardless of what your company values are, how can leaders bring them to life for your employees by sharing stories of what the values personally mean to them?

- Do you have a clear understanding of the different messages you need to share to the different audiences and know what stories to share with each?

- Would your team benefit from being educated in how to find and share stories more effectively?

CASE STORY
Transpower, New Zealand

Transpower New Zealand owns and operates the national grid that moves electricity from where it's generated to where it's consumed by homes and businesses. Their direct customers are large energy-generation and -distribution companies, but their work touches the lives of nearly every New Zealander.

Since its inception, Transpower operated from the simple and noble vision of 'Keeping the Lights On'. However, in 2016 Transpower was facing an unprecedented level of change in the electricity industry driven by new technologies, changing patterns of energy consumption and distribution, and growing demand for action to combat climate change.

With all this uncertainty in the business environment there was a growing concern that their employees were not fully prepared, or engaged, to meet the challenges and opportunity ahead. An employee engagement survey, conducted in 2016, showed employees were not engaged with their work, with the engagement score sitting at only 62 per cent.

Transpower knew its success would depend on their workforce being able to adapt and contribute in ways that could achieve the organisation's strategic goals. More importantly, Transpower wanted its people to know they—and their work—mattered.

Transpower also wanted to better reflect the country it served by creating a more diverse workforce. The electricity industry in New Zealand was traditionally one of male engineers and linesmen, so they designed information-gathering sessions to gain the perspectives of women and under-represented voices. This allowed people across the organisation to have a voice to help define the organisation's direction and culture for the years ahead.

Focus groups held at their offices across the country identified a general confusion created by years of competing communications messages and campaigns.

Head of Communications Rebecca Wilson explained,

> *There was a real disconnect between our internal brand and purpose and our external one—we needed clarity in communication and a clear sense of purpose and meaning in our work.*

Transpower's strategy, purpose and objectives were changing to meet the needs of the energy industry, a nation and its people, but its employees were still thinking 'we just keep the lights on'.

Transpower needed to find the heart and soul of its brand.

Who defines your brand?

It's at this point that many organisations turn to external consultants to define who they are. Transpower was no different; they hired a contractor and external consultancy to initially lead the work. They pushed for a central 'why' across the business: it was needed to enable Transpower's people to find a clear line of sight between what they do every day and how it relates to the organisation's purpose and objectives.

The consultancy held interviews across the business before delivering a proposal for a top-to-bottom rebrand of the company. They delivered a splashy presentation that made people stand up and take notice, but when it was tested beyond management it fell flat. It wasn't a disaster, according to Rebecca, but it missed the mark.

So they went back to the drawing board. They weren't interested in a 'rebranding for rebranding's sake' exercise. Employees had been through value rollouts before and were becoming tired of various corporate videos. They wanted to find a way to not only bring their brand, purpose and values to life but also keep them alive.

Enter Chris Dutton

Chris was the Senior Digital Communications Advisor for Transpower and worked closely with Rebecca on this project. Chris's background in marketing and communications meant he was always on the lookout for stories he could link to products his company was selling.

Chris echoed Rebecca's comments that there was little alignment between the message that was being communicated internally to employees and what was being communicated externally to its customers.

What the consultancy proposed didn't feel authentic. Chris and Rebecca knew that no-one could tell Transpower's story as well as their own people. They needed to reconsider their approach and, due to the tight budget and time frames involved, they decided to move the project management, copywriting, and creative direction in-house. The consultancy remained attached but turned their focus to developing session content for the leadership conference.

Rebecca and Chris quickly developed a strategic, integrated engagement communications project to be launched at a leadership conference in 90 days. It was expected to engage hearts and minds, but also provide the key information necessary to convey critical operational goals. And it all had to be done on a shoestring budget.

SUCCESS OF THE PROJECT WOULD BE MEASURED BY AUDIENCE REACTION AT THE LEADERSHIP CONFERENCE, EASE OF UNDERSTANDING OF KEY CONTENT, AND A LIFT IN THE EMPLOYEE ENGAGEMENT SCORE.

What gets you out of bed in the morning?

Sometimes we ask the metaphorical questions of what gets you out of bed each morning, but Rebecca said that, when you work for a company that owns the national electricity grid, you are often asked to come into work at 2 am when problems occur.

Rebecca wanted Chris to conduct one-on-one sessions with senior leaders, influencers and cynics in the business to hear the voice of Transpower's people, for himself, so he could come up with an alternative to what had been proposed. He began by travelling to Transpower's five offices across New Zealand to engage employees by asking them to contribute to what was being developed. He started by asking:

- What makes you most excited about your work?

- What role do you feel like you play in New Zealand society?

- What worries or excites you most about the future?

At the very end of the session he asked the simple question, 'Why do you come to work each day?' The sessions were held with small groups of people, with Chris staying on to speak individually to those who had more to say.

Rebecca said that the pleasing aspect of what they heard in those focus groups was the consistency in themes. Even though people would word it differently from 'keeping the lights on', the themes were still around serving New Zealanders:

- to make sure people's houses are warm in winter

- to make sure people can make breakfast before work

- to power jobs

- to make Aotearoa (New Zealand) a more sustainable society

- to be there for our neighbours.

After gathering this information, they went about creating the brand. They realised the company's 'why' couldn't be invented … and it certainly couldn't be outsourced. They realised that all they needed to do was to reflect the spirit of their people rather than try to tell them or sell them something new.

Chris and Rebecca looked again at what people were telling them and identified a 'why' that immediately struck a chord: 'We're for New Zealand.'

Representing the spirit

While Transpower's people were for New Zealand, they felt as a company they couldn't authentically reflect that sentiment unless they also spoke to representatives of Aotearoa's Indigenous people, the Māori. This ended up being a defining decision.

They consulted with *tangata whenua*, the people of the land, to explore how they may be able to appropriately represent the spirit of We're for New Zealand in Te Reo Māori, the language of *tangata whenua*. It was with the help of Māori that 'TūMai Aotearoa' was identified as the appropriate translation of 'We're for New Zealand'. 'Tū Mai Aotearoa', translated, means 'stand together New Zealand' or 'stand with me New Zealand'.

To be certain they were on the right track, Chris went back to some of those who had participated in the focus groups and tested the new 'why' against early alternatives presented by the external consultancy, including:

- Turn on New Zealand

- Powering New Zealand

- We're for New Zealand *Tū Mai Aotearoa*

Even the cynics had a clear preference and it proved they were headed in the right direction. Moving project management, creative direction, copywriting and video direction in-house ensured they could effectively devote more resources to external graphic design and production of collaterals. This allowed Transpower to economically create a high-quality look and feel that would engage its audience through a more human connection, rather than using the images of wires and towers that had previously dominated their communication.

Their 'why' was about their people. So, it was important that anything they developed engaged people on a human level.

One week before the leadership conference, the session content had not yet been delivered and the external consultancy quit—leaving Transpower's contractor, Rebecca and Chris to finish the project. Two days before the start of the conference they put the finishing touches on all the material.

Show it again

A professional-quality video was produced to introduce Tū Mai Aotearoa. This video was aired on the first day of the leadership conference as part of a presentation delivered by members of the general management team. Subsequent presentations over the next day and a half were all designed to reflect the why. At the conference, each people leader engaged their peers in exercises to explore how they, their teams and the company all embodied Tū Mai Aotearoa.

Each attendee at the conference was also provided with a large, A5 printed book that included a new, unified and simplified internal brand identity. Additionally, this book included their One Framework, a learning device that provided an easily digestible visual representation of the why, the company's behaviours, mission statement and the six strategic priorities.

Most importantly, they clearly displayed how these items linked and were dependent on each other, as well as the content of Tū Mai Aotearoa.

Rebecca and Chris delivered the first stage of the project on time and on budget. But the real measure of success was how Tū Mai Aotearoa would be received. The video at the leadership conference received an overwhelmingly positive response. Chris said, 'The video received loud applause, with several audience members tearing up as they watched.' They were absolutely blown away with the response when, after a short break, a second showing of the video was requested by the attendees.

People leaders were quick to understand how the 'why' influenced them, their work, and why it was important to take the necessary steps to prepare for the future—so much so that they began running exercises immediately following the leadership conference, before the formal launch of Tū Mai Aotearoa.

Once it was released to the people managers at the leadership conference, they then introduced Tū Mai Aotearoa at each office through presentations given by the Chief Executive. People managers used the materials they'd developed to run further exercises with their teams, as well as to develop quarterly goals for individual employees.

Company-wide, Tū Mai Aotearoa proved to be somewhat of an awakening for staff. People began using Tū Mai Aotearoa to explain how their work and projects would help the company better meet New Zealand's future electricity needs.

The general management team were quick to recognise how invested their employees were in Tū Mai Aotearoa and decided to incorporate it in their new corporate headquarters as it was being built. The tagline appeared with graphic elements from the campaign on frosted meeting room windows throughout the building, Waikoukou, when it opened in 2017.

Three months later they conducted their employee engagement survey with an independent outside company, Aon Hewitt. They achieved an employee engagement score of 75 per cent, a 13 per cent lift in their score from the previous year. Which is an impressive result.

BUT THE USE OF STORIES DIDN'T JUST END WITH A NEW TAGLINE AND PROFESSIONAL CORPORATE VIDEO.

Being on the lookout for stories

During the earlier focus groups and interviews, Chris had kept hearing interesting stories. He knew from his marketing career that while stories are powerful to sell a product, they are also powerful to sell a message. In this case, the company's strategic priorities, which were:

- play an active role in shaping the industry's future

- develop our organisational effectiveness

- improve our asset management

- reduce costs and evolve our service to remain competitive

- match our infrastructure to need over time

- sustain our social licence to operate.

There was clarity on what the stories needed to communicate and demonstrate; he just needed to find the them. He started to dig deeper to find a variety of stories that could reinforce the intent behind the six strategic priorities. He thought it would be useful to 'create a collective narrative'.

I've come to dislike the word 'narrative' over the years because it has been overused and often unnecessarily used ... a bit like 'journey'. But Chris's use of 'narrative' is appropriate. A narrative is a lot of stories that together paint a bigger picture. Each of the stories can stand alone but form part of a larger narrative. Like a piece of a jigsaw puzzle.

Chris acknowledged he was in a 'very privileged position'. He gained close access to the senior leadership team and would visit various sites across Transpower to uncover these precious stories. He was the story detector.

Knowing this is not as easy as you would think, I was interested in how Chris went about it. He said it was critical that

> for people to share stories with you, you need to build credibility. You need to spend a lot of time listening, asking good questions and looking for a human connection.

Like my metal detector analogy, Chris was asking the right questions, listening and forever looking for when to dig beneath the sand.

During this story-finding process Chris uncovered some powerful stories that would form part of the overarching narrative he was hoping for.

For example, in this 'story detector' mode Chris found out about two young employees who were working on drones. Chris detected a potential story that would be valuable to share and started to dig a bit deeper. He found out that this was not only a great story about the innovative technology being explored but it would also tie into a 'diversity of thought' strategy they were also implementing.

In an industry that is very much male-dominated by seasoned workers, here were two young employees using machine learning and algorithms to lead the way. One of the employees, a female engineer, represented part of the new future Transpower was hoping to help shape: a world with more Māori and young women in STEM (Science, Technology, Engineering and Mathematics) careers.

Another story was the Northland outage incident, discussed in part II.

The ripple effect of stories

Like Tū Mai Aotearoa, these stories were all made into videos and shared widely. Externally, they shared the videos on their website and social media channels. Internally they shared the videos as part of the Chief Executive's weekly video and email to all employees. They also disseminated the videos in the news feed on their intranet.

In the company's lobby at their head office building, in Wellington, the videos are featured as part of their interactive wall, where visitors can explore key moments in Transpower's history. This is the prominent feature that welcomes all clients, suppliers, employees and guests into the building.

Such was the impact of these stories that they gained interest from traditional media channels, with national broadcasters carrying stories on Transpower and its enabling role in the decarbonisation of New Zealand's economy, as well as its use of drones and robots. The Tū Mai Aotearoa story was featured in traditional print media, as well as on TV.

What was pleasing, and shows the power of the ripple effect of a good story, is that Transpower's partners also started sharing the videos. For example, their subcontractors would share the Tū Mai Aotearoa and Māori and Cultural Heritage Site videos internally to their employees as part of their training programs. The University of Canterbury also used

Transpower's Women in Technology video to promote the university's program for female secondary school STEM students—and also to help raise awareness with potential corporate partners. Ngāti Rangi, an iwi from the central North Island, shared the Rangataua Lakes video with iwi leaders, and the Department of Conservation used it for social media.

The integrated communications and engagement strategy extended also to using Tū Mai Aotearoa and the connected narrative to reshape the company's induction program. The two-day session was re-focused around the company's people and their stories to help weave together the experience and voices of employees old and new.

SEVERAL VIDEOS ARE SHOWN DURING THE INDUCTION, WITH ACTIVITIES DESIGNED AROUND ALLOWING NEW EMPLOYEES TO SHARE THEIR OWN STORIES TO CONNECT TO THE COMPANY'S PURPOSE AND VALUES.

Check and reflect

- Do you have consistency and clarity on the messages being communicated?

- Have you involved employees in what the brand should be?

- Are there stories you could turn into videos to allow you to share them widely, such as on social media or in the lobby of your building?

- Is there an opportunity to share stories that will support you and potentially your partners?

- Do you have dedicated people who know how to discover these stories in your organisation?

- Could you use the catalyst of perhaps an anniversary or new building or new logo to actively find relevant stories?

Conclusion

My hope for you in reading this book is that you have gained three things:

1. **Clarity** around what brand storytelling is (and isn't) and the power of sharing magnetic stories.

2. **Knowledge** to implement brand storytelling into your own organisation.

3. **Inspiration** from what others have achieved by investing in brand storytelling.

No organisation is too small or too large to implement brand storytelling.

Remember: your brand is the stories people share about you, so I encourage you to take greater control of that. Be clear on what your brand is and know how it's influenced by the stories you proactively communicate and by what you do, which also creates stories.

As Tyrion Lannister said in the final episode of *Game of Thrones*, 'What unites people? Armies? Gold? Flags? Stories. There's nothing in the world more powerful than a good story. Nothing can stop it. No enemy can defeat it.'[1]

So what magnetic stories will you share from now on?

---

[1] Full disclosure: I have never watched an episode of *Game of Thrones*, but during that final episode I had about twenty people send me a text about this quote.

Connect with me

If you have connected with this book, then I would love for us to connect. It's always a pleasure as an author to hear from people on what insights and inspiration they took from the book.

I work globally and virtually, so if you and/or your company want a bit more hands-on help implementing brand storytelling, then I would love to hear from you. If you would like me to train your leaders in storytelling or speak at your next conference then simply drop me an email.

You can also access my seven-day storytelling starter kit from my website, which is, as the name suggests, a kit that will get you started with storytelling!

And if you like this book you may like my previous books, especially *Stories for Work* and *Real Communication*.

You might also like to listen to my podcast called *Authentic Leadership*, where I interview business leaders on all things leadership and communication. It's available on iTunes and SoundCloud.

The best ways to get in touch and stay connected are:

Email — gabrielle@gabrielledolan.com

Websites — gabrielledolan.com & jargonfreefridays.com

LinkedIn — gabrielledolan

Instagram — gabrielledolan.1

Facebook — gabrielledolanconsulting

Twitter — GabrielleDolan1

Podcast — *Authentic Leadership*

YouTube — Gabrielle Dolan

Index

Also available from Gabrielle Dolan ...

Available in print, audio and e-book formats

Also available from Gabrielle Dolan ...

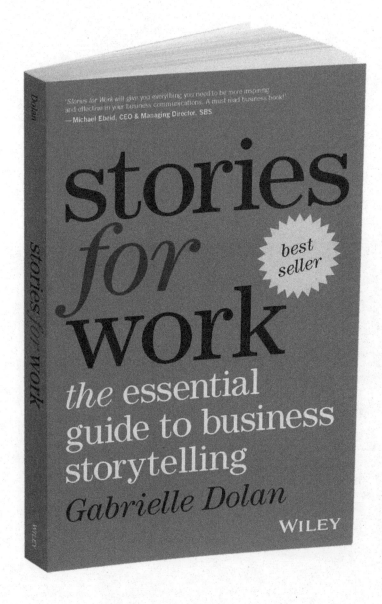

Available in print, audio and e-book formats

Printed in Australia
05 Aug 2024
LP033675